Opportunities in the Gap Year

SIXTEENTH EDITION

Edited by Philip Gray

Careerscope Guides
ISBN 0 901936 99 5
April 2005

www.careerscope.info

Design: Philip Gray

Text set in Georgia 9 on 11pt

Print: Print Solutions Partnership

(c) CAREERSCOPE GUIDES 2005

12A Princess Way, Camberley, Surrey GUI5 3SP
Tel: 01276 21188   Fax: 01276 691833
Email: sylvie.pool@isco.org.uk
www.careerscope.info

First published January 1969
Sixteenth edition April 2005

CONTENTS

Time to take a break

Options

You've just received you're A level results - now you can do what you want. Jackarooing on a farm in the Australian outback? No problem. Becoming a diving instructor in Thailand? Step this way! School is over, and a world of new experiences awaits you - all you need to do is decide what to do next. Whether heading abroad or staying in the UK, the opportunities are endless.

Recharge your batteries

Recent increases in the cost of higher education have put the spotlight on the year out and students are questioning whether heading straight into university is a better idea. Before rushing on to university and into the world of work, stop for a moment. This is your best chance to take some time out, recharge your batteries and pick up some memories that may look better on the mantelpiece of old age than all those dusty certificates. You can easily make the money to pay for a truly memorable year out. In fact, there are lots of ways you can fund your travels when on the road and even head off to university with a healthy looking bank account.

Isobel Franks is a great example of how to make the best out of your year out. She worked at a Yorkshire sports kit company to raise funds, went on a project to Argentina, then finished off her time out with travel in Europe and work back in Yorkshire before heading to the University of Durham where she is now studying biology.

Potential benefits

Anthony McClaran, Chief Executive of UCAS has this to say about Gap Years: "We at UCAS believe that by adding the experience of a planned year out to their qualifications students actively

BSES Expeditions

improve their chances of successfully completing a course." Quite simply, experience complements education. Universities and colleges widely recognise the potential benefits of taking a year out which, when well organised, extend into later life.

You'll be in good company on a gap year: well over 30,000 students deferred entry to university last year, and one fifth of all tourism journeys in the world are made by young travellers.

Taking a year out is seen as being a positive thing by employers, too. A gap year can give you the edge in all sorts of situations. The world may be full of opportunities, but it's also a hugely competitive place. Thousands of people just like you are after that place at university, that work experience placement to die for and that job at the end of it.

Taking a gap year and equipping yourself with new skills and experiences is a great way to make your application rise magically to the top of the pile: "I found myself with so much to say on job applications, and answers to so many tricky questions in interviews. Practical experience and hands-on challenges made a huge difference to how confident I felt when applying for jobs", says Mark Andrews, a history graduate from Keele.

There's nothing like being in an unfamiliar situation and trying your hand at new skills to expand your horizons. After a change of scene and incredibly different challenges, heading into university with lots of people just like you will seem a breeze. Meeting new people from around the world will increase your confidence and make the first week at university a lot less daunting.

Of course, gap years need to be carefully planed financially. Possibly for the first time, you really take control of your finances and know how much money you need to pay for an expedition, an airfare and your living costs.

Life-changing experience
For Chris Parker, his adventure into the unknown was to take him to the remote Arctic wilderness of Svalbard with BSES. Away from home comforts, friends and family, he initially found the experience daunting: "I soon got over my worries when I realised what an amazing place I was now living in." He found upon return he'd developed a "greater independence" and bounced into university with enthusiasm for challenges ahead.

Ultimately, taking time out to work, travel or join an expedition has the potential to be a life-changing experience; as Alison Sargeant says "You really learn to evaluate what matters in life and what isn't worth worrying about."

What are you waiting for?

The full version of this article, by Tom Hall, was recently published in Careerscope Magazine at www.careerscope.info

Paying your way

Gap years can be expensive, whether you go on an expedition, travel or decide to boost your skills in other areas. Don't let this put you off - there are pleanty of ways you can have an unforgettable year out, boost your CV and leave your bank balance looking rosy.

Career building
Numerous companies in the UK offer year-out placements where you're getting hands-on experience that can be invaluable in building a career. Chris Edmunds spent a year out with KPMG, which led to an offer of a full-time position. "I got a first foot in the door, met people from all over the company and got a real understanding for how the business works", he says.

Venture Co

"I loved the responsibility and knowledge that I was furthering my career." If you're planning to study or work in engineering, science or technology then the Year in Industry (www.yini.org.uk) will be right up your street. With 30 years of experience of interesting, challenging placements for young people, you can earn up to £12,000 in a year on top of all the valuable skills and contacts this will bring.

Of course, if you know what area you'd like to work in it's quite possible to approach companies yourself - armed with a CV, determination and a willingness to work hard you can work in pretty much any area you choose.

There are also lots of ways to top up your funds when you're on the road. A common tactic is to pause a while in Australia or New Zealand, both of which operate popular working holiday visa schemes. Generally you are allowed to work for periods of up to three months with the same employer - the idea being that you are supplementing travel funds. This is a popular option and in big cities like Sydney and Melbourne competition is fierce, but there's plenty of work available up and down the country.

Hostels need staff; fruit needs to be picked and beers need to served. If you are flexible and keen, there's no reason why this can't be a profitable part of your trip.

The full version of this article, by Tom Hall, was recently published in Careerscope Magazine at www.careerscope.info

The value of volunteering

When you start to think about taking a gap year it's highly likely that you'll consider the idea of some form of voluntary work, usually abroad. But think again, voluntary work doesn't have to be linked to foreign travel - there are plenty of options on your doorstep. Making the most of them, either in conjunction with a paying job while you raise money for a big trip, or as the focus of your year out, is one of the great opportunities of a gap year.

If you're interested in getting into social work or conservation as a career, volunteering can give you an invaluable insight into these fields as well as provide you with the necessary experience that future employers will demand. Even if you're not drawn to this type of career, the fact that you've volunteered shows commitment, a generosity of spirit and a willingness to throw yourself into different environments - all of which looks excellent on your CV.

Volunteer agencies

The UK's largest volunteer and training agency, Community Service Volunteers (www.csv.org.uk), organises the Millennium Volunteers scheme (www.mvonline.gov.uk) which is aimed solely at 16 to 24-year-olds.

In exchange for helping the local community in some way - anything from getting involved in the local theatre to helping to run a sexual health programme - you get the chance to develop your skills and

BTCV

personal qualities and add something really wonhwhile to your CV.

Another good place to look is Timebank (www.timebank.org. uk). a national campaign to encourage volunteering in your local community. Timebank has numerous contacts, plenty of advice and a hefty dose of inspiration. Alternatively, try Volunteering England (www. volunteering.org.uk).

WWW (WorldWide Volunteering; www.worldwidevolunteering.org.uk) operate a database with nearly 1,000 volunteer organisations and can match up your specific requirements to one of these organisations. As the name suggests, their remit goes beyond the UK, but there are plenty of opportunities available in Britain, with activities as diverse as scrub clearance on a Scottish island to taking a group of disabled youngsters on their first holiday to the coast.

If you're keen to work in the environment, an ideal place to start is with the British Trust for Conservation Volunteers (www. btcv.org), the UK's leading charity working with people to bring about environmental change - primarily in the UK but also abroad.

Over 10,000 people aged between 16 and 24 years old are already involved with BTCV, which has opportunities ranging from getting dirty for one day while you help rebuild a footpath to working as a long-term volunteer on anything from managing other

BTCV

volunteers on conservation holidays to helping with publicity campaigns and organising events.

Worthwhile work

Volunteering is a significant commitment to make, whatever you choose to do, so talk to as many people as possible and think about it carefully before you commit - especially if it's for a longer period of time or you're going to be involved in any kind of social work.

Volunteering not only gives you skills, contacts, experience and confidence, it also gives you an opportunity to do something really worthwhile by giving your time to other people or the environment. **And that's definitely a feeling money can't buy.**

The full version of this article, by Imogen Franks, was recently published in Careerscope Magazine at www.careerscope.info

Sporting passions

Peak Leaders

If you've got a real passion for the outdoors and you're determined to make a career out of it, you can use your Gap Year as a way to combine travel with getting some essential skills. The challenge of mountaineering, the thrill of winter sports and the graceful teamwork of sailing are all examples of how mastering an activity can pave the way for a career and give you skills you can pass on to others - anywhere in the world.

Learn abroad

"I was keen to master the skills needed to climb in the Alps so I'd have more experience to lead groups in the UK." The idea of clinging precariously to a rock face thousands of metres above a Swiss village is not everyone's idea of fun but for Julia Fea it was heaven: Julia's long term aim was to lead mountaineering tours worldwide, and she was building on previous experience: "I'd done several mountaineering courses in the UK, so this was a case of applying what I'd learnt there to a new, more challenging environment."

Julia took part in the Alpine Climbing course run by Plas Y Brenin (www. pyb.co.uk), the UK National Mountain Centre. They organise a wide range of courses aimed at improving mountain craft and offer everything from advice to formal qualifications.

With the growing popularity of working as a ski or snowboard instructor, it's a great idea to pick up some experience before trying your hand working at a resort. The more qualified you are, the greater your chances of beating the competition to your chosen job, whether as a winter sports professional or transfering your skills to another vocation.

As aspiring pro riders know only too well, the UK isn't the ideal place for learning the skills needed on the slopes. Increasing numbers are heading abroad to do just this. Mhairi Hughes (pictured laft, centre) traded a warm European summer for two months in snowy Argentina with Peak Leaders (www.peakleaders.com).

Despite being in the middle of a degree, Mhairi had no hesitation in opting for this course rather than getting some work experience: "The course was just as relevant and beneficial as a stint gaining work experience at a big company. I learnt the value of working to a common goal, team-building exercises and multi-tasking." The course also gave Mhairi some great qualifications: "By the end I was a certified Canadian snowboard instructor, I had a first aid certificate, avalanche training, a UK management and leadership award, a suntan and the best summer in between university terms yet!"

Duke of Edinburgh Award

By now, the Duke of Edinburgh award (www.theaward.org) may be a very familiar subject, and many of you will have got involved to some degree.

Although you can start from the age of 14, you can still begin the award until you are 18. If you're in the middle of it, there is a huge variety of overseas trips that you can take that will count towards your award.

A popular option is to take part in a project through an organisation like World Challenge Expeditions (www.world-challenge.co.uk) as part of your final Gold Award. They offer everything from a two week tip to Morocco to a nine month conservation education placement in Tanzania.

Opportunities galore

The more knowledge you can get on your chosen specialisation, the more you'll get out of it. Joe Simpson's Touching The Void is a classic tale of mountaineering - and a gripping read. Sailing nuts are sure to enjoy Ellen Macarthur's Taking On The World, an account of her solo yachting experience. There are opportunities to master surfing in Hawaii, lifesaving in Australia, windsurfing in Greece, jungle survival in Borneo, orienteering in Finland, gliding in the USA, and much much more.

Doing any of these can open doors to seeing the world and picking up abilities, interests and friends to stand you in good stead way beyond your gap year.

The full version of this article, by Tom Hall, was recently published in Careerscope Magazine at www.careerscope.info

Expedition experiences

In terms of learning new skills and languages, meeting people from around the world and really getting under the skin of a country heading off on an expedition takes some beating. An expedition will generally be organised through an established company and you'll need to raise funds to take part. Beyond that, you can go pretty much anywhere and get involved in a huge variety of projects.

Choosing an expedition

Of course, a universe of choice presents its own problems. How on earth do you choose what to do and who to do it with? A good starting point is to look for a project, organisation or destination that matches your future educational or career goals. Damien Rickwood chose a project that fitted in with his study plans and interests, joining a Trekforce conservation project which combined environmental work with learning Spanish. He's now studying French and Spanish at Sheffield University. The experience was immensely rewarding, he describes it as: "The biggest adventure of my life – becoming a teaching Tarzan, learning to dive, sunrises a-top ancient temples, climbing volcanoes and more!"

Thorough research

Being fully briefed about where you are going and what you're doing will help avoid problems. Think and research hard when it comes to choosing your trip: we're talking about a lot of money. If you can, get a second opinion from parents or friends.

Expeditions cover the world and offer a huge amount of choice. One of the best-known organisations is Raleigh International, who organise expeditions to Chile, Costa Rica & Nicaragua, Ghana, Namibia, Sabah-

Venbture Co

Borneo and Fiji. Groups are comprised of volunteers from host countries, disadvantaged backgrounds in the UK, Gap Year workers and young people from other countries making for a brilliant cultural mix.

If you fancy three and a half months in the Arctic wilderness, BSES Expeditions offer trips to Svalbard, Norway and Greenland as well as a number of more conventional destinations including Peru, South Africa and Chile. Alison Sargeant loved her scientific research trip to the far north, especially "the awesome scale and sheer beauty of this Arctic wilderness".

Catherine Speller's adventure took her teaching in Nepal with Student Projects Worldwide. She quickly gained the skills she needed to do the job: "It's amazing what four weeks of training, some emergency gold stars and several prayers heavenward can do". Bringing lessons learnt in the playground at home to a new country meant she could pass on lessons in a fun and informative way. Catherine came to terms with working in a developing country and learnt to work through problems: "Things happen slowly in Nepal – it can be slow, frustrating and exhausting. But I can't stress enough how important the experience was for me."

Cross Cultural Solutions offer the chance to work on sustainable development programmes side-by-side with local people. They offer a shorter than average but in-depth connection to the country you're visiting. Jennifer

Tam went to Guatemala, working with abandoned and abused children. She found that the country was friendly and welcoming, she was able to learn Spanish and given cause to want to volunteer further.

Fellow volunteer Emma Bird visited Peru. She says: "It was surprising, especially to a reserved English girl, how quickly bonds were formed between the volunteers – so much that spending time with each other felt like spending time with family."

The variety offered by i-to-i was what appealed to Emma Kirby: "I did three, three-week conservation projects in Ecuador which was brilliant, as it enabled us to experience a greater diversity of people, lifestyle and environment – coast, jungle and rain forest – than we would have encountered on one project." Emma also had time off between projects to travel and brush up on her languages.

The full version of this article, by Tom Hall, was recently published in Careerscope Magazine at www.careerscope.info

Venture Co

Options

Brushing up your language skills

Imagine being asked to give a speech on the opening of a building you and your team have built in a remote African village. Your newly-acquired Swahili skills enable you to make a great speech and the whole group is proud of you.

Picture an alternative scene - you're waiting for a bus in Peru when a group of students come up to you. They're keen to chat, and you're keen to talk, but lack the Spanish. After trying for a while they give up and happen on another backpacker who can chat away in Spanish. He gets invited on a cultural trip to an undiscovered village, while you miss out.

Got the picture yet? Languages open doors and break down barriers. Make yourself heard and you'll get so much more out of your trip. You can close that cultural gap much faster if you're seen to be making an effort.

Changing perceptions

The most straightforward languages to learn will be ones that you've already studied. Jol Attwoll headed to Guatemala to take part in rural development work for six months and then travel on through South America. He travelled to some of Central America's most isolated areas, doing heavy physical labour and some office work.

Upon arrival, AFS (www.afs.org), who organised the trip, sent Jol on a Spanish course. "Learning the language helped in all the obvious ways. By the end of my stay I was able to have a half-decent conversation with people and find out a lot more about Guatemala's troubled history than I could have done with Spanglish sign language."

Jol also found that speaking Spanish changed people's perceptions of him: "People appreciate you making the effort, even if you're struggling with some words and phrases. You're not viewed as a mad gringo, but someone who wants to find out about their lives and help out. "

Jol put his language skills to use, going on to work for an English language newspaper and teaching English and French in Santiago, Chile. "I couldn't have done those jobs without a working knowledge of Spanish, nor would I have even thought of going for them."

Enrol on a course

Sometimes it's necessary to learn as much as you can before setting out. Ted Franks spent a summer in Morocco on an International Volunteer Project run by UNA Exchange (www.unexchange.org).

"I knew French would be the dominant language on the project, and took a week-long intensive course at the Institute Français in London. They run courses for all levels and it's a great environment to learn in," says Ted.

CIEE

"By the time I got out there I was raring to go. Without it I'd have struggled, especially during the getting-to-know-you stage. By the end, my colleagues on the trip were very impressed with how my French had developed." Of course, any language looks great on your CV, especially if you've learnt it off your own back.

Getting your head round a language you may not have run into before is an extra challenge, but one which has its own rewards. Anthony Buchan spent a year in Tanzania and learnt the basics of Swahili while on a project for his first three months there: "Learning the basics of the language was the most important thing I did. It opened up numerous

opportunities to me. It ensured that you were welcomed in far more than the average tourist. As it's not a language that is widely known or spoken in other parts of the world it was a pleasure for locals to meet foreigners who had made an effort, however small."

After three months on the conservation project with Frontier (www.frontier.ac.uk), Anthony decided to try and stay on in Tanzania. The difference between success and failure of this idea was the Swahili he'd picked up. "I got work at a privately run marine park as an education officer and environmental engineer working alongside Tanzanians who spoke very little or no English. Without a knowledge of Swahili this would not have been feasible." There'll be language courses available in most places you go to, or if not, you'll be able to swap English conversation for a lesson in the local language. Try to take a dictionary and a phrasebook in case you get stuck. However, some languages are more straightforward than others.

Chris Mills spent six weeks surfing in Bali as part of his Gap Year round-the-world trip, where he picked up Bahasa Indonesia surprisingly easily. "For the beginner, Indonesian is perfect. It has genderless grammar, phonetic spelling and a great learning environment. The Balinese were very considerate and slowed down the pace of their speech to help me out." He found people very happy to swap lessons with him. Picking up Indonesian also had an unexpected benefit: 'I was there for the surfing, and fell into conversation asking some local surfers about the best breaks.

The next day they took me off to some amazing places where there weren't other surfers - still the best memory of my trip." If that's not enough to convince you, fellow travellers will admire and be curious about your new-found language skills - another way to make friends on the road.

Check all your options
Of course, there are plenty of other worthwhile courses that will give you excellent skills you can apply back home. A Teaching English as a Foreign Language certificate (www.bielt.org or www.tefl.com for more) can allow you to work almost anywhere you go. Other popular courses include yoga, art, cookery and cultural studies. Pick your destination, get in touch with a local university or other institution and find out what your options are.

Just because you're on a break from education doesn't mean you should stop learning!

The full version of this article, by Tom Hall, was recently published in Careerscope Magazine at www.careerscope.info

CESA Languages Abroad

Into Africa

Africa is huge in every way – and you shouldn't miss it. Africa stretches over nearly 19 million square miles and is home to 750 million people who speak thousands of languages. It has the wastes of the Sahara Desert, the amazing Rift Valley, open savannahs and tropical jungles.

It's an incredible place to visit and an even more remarkable one to be based in for a few months. If you go, Africa will leave an indelible impression like nowhere else. The possibilities for what to do there are varied and well organised. Africa has many problems, but if your dominant image of the place is of desperate poverty you'll have your conceptions challenged by the beautiful landscape, friendly people and amazing diversity.

A safe place to visit

Many travellers are put off visiting Africa due to safety and health concerns. In reality, it's generally a safe and welcoming place to visit. For your first visit it's a good idea to think about going on an organised trip or truck. Of course, there are some no-go areas, and you need to be on your guard in big cities. Prepare by doing some research, and exercise common sense. As with anywhere, you shouldn't leave home without travel insurance.

The Suzy Lamplugh Trust (www. suzylamplugh.org) has some excellent advice on safe travel available.

A popular way for young people to see Africa for the first time is on an overland truck. These adventure tours are run by companies like Guerba (www.guerba.co.uk) and Dragoman (www.dragoman.co.uk), who offer safe and organised transportation in a social, fun environment. Popular trips involve multiweek journeys from Nairobi in Kenya to Johannesburg or Cape Town, but there are many different routes available.

The group decides on what to see and do, giving the trips a real team atmosphere. Often you'll pay to get on the trip, and then need to provide your own airfare and contribute to the kitty for meals and drinks. Travelling this way avoids many of the stresses of African travel, including getting visas, dealing with officialdom and using public transport, which can all be frustrating experiences. Trucks aren't for everyone however – you can't tell in advance if everyone will get on, and the vehicles attract a lot of attention.

Variety of work

South Africa offers the chance to find a variety of work. Charlie Watson spent a couple of months waitressing in Cape Town, after travelling there with Bunac (www.bunac.org). "I found Cape Town a great place to spend a while. The cost of living is low and I was able to survive on tips and put a bit away. After working, I took a trip up to Kruger National Park and saw some more of the country. Looking back, it was great to be there at this time in the country's history." South Africa is very well set up for independent backpacking too, with companies like the Baz Bus (www. bazbus.com) offering tours.

No trip to Africa would be complete without going on safari and trying to see the "big five" – lion, leopard, elephant, rhino and wildebeest. Seeing these beasts in their (often spectacular) natural environment is an incredibly moving experience that shouldn't be missed. There are dozens of national parks and game reserves all over East and Southern Africa that offer a wide range of safari – but you need to choose carefully which one to visit.

Before handing over any money, find out how many other people there'll be in your group, what accommodation and food is included and how long you'll spend looking at animals as opposed to driving to and from the park. Imogen Franks loved her safari

experience: "Going to the Masai Mara in Kenya was amazing, but it was crowded with other safari groups – you may see less animals in a more remote park, but it will be more personal and memorable."

There are endless opportunities for project work in Africa. Everything from community work with Christian organisations to West African monkey sanctuaries is possible. It is the perfect place to get involved in conservation. Companies like Greenforce (www.greenforce.org) organise many projects. It's a great chance to work closely with qualified biologists in a structured, educational but informal environment.

Spending time in Africa as part of your Gap Year could be one of the best things you ever do.

The full version of this article, by Tom Hall, was recently published in Careerscope Magazine at www.careerscope.info

Biosphere Expeditions

Eco Africa Experience

Options

Australasian adventure

BUNAC

This diverse part of the world attracts thousands of gap year students each year, and with very good reason. Whether it is the appeal of cosmopolitan Sydney, the lure of the great outdoors in New Zealand or the chance to explore the different cultures of South East Asia, there's something for everyone and a good time is guaranteed.This part of the world has been catering for backpackers for many years and a trip here is usually hassle-free, fun-filled

and sun-soaked. Of course, as with anywhere in the world, this doesn't mean that you can leave your common sense at home. Take all the usual precautions, browse publications and websites for more advice - and check the planning organisations featured in the next section.

City work

Australia offers endless opportunities, whether you just want to travel around or you need to settle somewhere to get cash together to keep going. Sydney lives up to all expectations as a relaxed, beautiful city to live in, but you won't be the first person to discover this and you may find your chances of getting work are greater in Melbourne, Cairns or Brisbane.

In the cities it's relatively easy to get work especially if you have basic administrative skills or experience in the catering industry. More challenging jobs are available as well but it all depends on whether you want to get work experience for your career or just money for the next stage of your trip.

A good way of making money and seeing more of the great Australian outdoors is to take a job on a farm, either fruit picking (which can work very well if you get a good team together) or even following in Prince Harry's footsteps as a jackeroo or jillaroo.

The Australians operate a Working Holiday Visa that makes it easy for British citizens aged between 18 and 30 to get work so take advantage of it! If you fancy doing something worthwhile with your time here, there's plenty of conservation work or organic farms crying out for support. And of course no trip to Australia is complete without exploring the main highlights of this diverse and fascinating country, including the magnificent Ulhuru and the beautiful Great Barrier Reef.

Airline routes
Most round-the-world tickets make a stop in South East Asia almost compulsory; it's also very easy to tag on a flight to New Zealand from Australia and a stop at one of those beautiful Pacific islands is easy to accommodate either inbound or outbound. Do your homework before you book your trip though, as once it's booked things are more difficult to change.

One popular route is to fly into Bangkok and then travel south before heading up north and through to Laos, Vietnam and Cambodia and then flying back out of Bangkok and onwards to your next destination. If you want to go further, you can do the same route and continue onto Australia via Malayasia, Singapore and the many islands of Indonesia before flying out of Bali which has excellent connections to Australia.

Working holiday visas
To get a working holiday visa for Australia or New Zealand you need to show that you have a certain amount of money in the bank and a valid onward ticket, so they know that you're not going to stay too long! For more information, check out www.immi.gov.au for Australia and www.immigration.govt.nz for New Zealand. Remember to give yourself enough time to get this organised as the visas can take a while to be issued and you don't want to arrive without it if you're intending to work while in either of these two countries.

The full version of this article, by Imogen Franks, was recently published in Careerscope Magazine at www.careerscope.info

North American horizons

Hollywood, New York, the Great Lakes, the Grand Canyon, the Appalachian Trail, Friends, Woodstock, the blues, Elvis, hip hop, Coca Cola: Just reel a few things you associate with the USA off the top of your head, and you quickly form an idea of America's staggering geographical, cultural and economical might. No wonder it exerts such a draw on people.

Work placements

The language is another obvious appeal for gap year travellers as well as a popular culture that most have been exposed to from a young age. But, there are some practicalities you need to consider before trying to realise your American dreams. Most importantly, the necessary USA entry process is complex, even for gap year travellers, only selected programmes qualify for entry, and extended working visas are hard to obtain. The easiest gap year options involve summer or seasonal work. But although these placements usually last for a maximum of four months, they offer a unique opportunity to sample a continent that, despite its constant presence on our TV screens, really needs to be seen first-hand.

Simon Harding, a law student at Liverpool University, worked as a kitchen hand in Berkshire Hills summer camp, close to the three-way border of Connecticut, New York and Massachusetts. For his job, he sliced countless bagels; he also gained an unforgettable insight into the American summer camp institution. "I thought I knew about America before," he says. "But a lot of things were different to how I expected." The money he received after the camp allowed him buy an Amtrak rail ticket and travel down to New Orleans with co-workers, calling in at Boston, Chicago, and Washington en route. If your A levels are looming, you may want to consider a placement in a North American high school after you finish. This is like a fast-track route to discovering the ethos and attitudes of the continent, as well as experiencing a different educational approach.

Full-time students may also be eligible for US internship programmes that directly relate to their studies. These positions can be paid or unpaid, depending on the field you are interested in.

Travel options

Almost everyone who works in the US will want to travel before they return home. To even scratch the US's vast surface, research your transport options thoroughly. As well as Amtrak, the ubiquitous Greyhound bus will take you most places. This is probably the cheapest travel option, although certainly not the quickest.

Canadian sights

Canada may be the lower profile of the North American countries, but it too offers some fantastic gap year opportunities. In pure square miles it actually outstrips its brasher southern neighbour, and is larger than China. Lakes, mountains, prairies, grasslands and waterfalls are all part of the breathtaking Canadian landscape. Previous gap year students describe the inhabitants as warm and laidback. In fact, the Canadian cultural mix is an intriguing one. French influences vie with its British colonial past, which in turn mingles with the nation's indigenous roots.

Sarah White, 19, is on a gap year work placement in the Canadian Rockies organised through BUNAC (www. bunac.co.uk). She is due to start her English literature course at the University of East Anglia, and is full of enthusiasm for her year out. She says she will miss everything about Canada "the mountains, snow, atmosphere, people, my job."

Other Canadian must-sees include the colonial architecture of the capital Ottawa; the European-style charm of Quebec City; the adventure tourism of British Colombia; the bilingual cultural diversity of Montreal; and the maritime appeal of Nova Scotia. In Yellowknife, intrepid travellers can also see the spectacular northern lights. From autumn through to the end of winter, this natural phenomenon streaks the skies with incredible hues of blue, green and red.

For further inspiration be sure to read On the Road by Jack Kerouac, a gripping depiction of the Beat Generation travel counter-culture that surged in America during the 1950s. Jon Krakauer's Into the Wild is a mesmerising account of a young man who tries to find himself and harness the secrets of the great American wilderness.

The full version of this article, by Jolyon Attwooll, was recently published in Careerscope Magazine at www.careerscope.info

What to take with you

Options

The right attitude: "take only photos, leave only footprints"

Mandatories: passport with relevant visa(s), airline tickets, foreign currency, travellers' cheques, insurance, credit card

Money belt: out of sight, out of thieves' hands. Wrap passport in plastic bag

Photocopies of passport pages: be safe, not sorry

Wallet: velcro fastener

Backpack: approx 55/60 litres for girls, 70/75 litres for boys

Daypack: 25 litres, so you can leave the big pack at the hostel

Old watch: if it gets wet, battered or stolen, then it doesn't matter

Travel alarm clock

Inner sheet: cotton/silk. Easy to wash, instead of an entire sleeping bag

Towel: Life Venture Trek Towel XL. Very compact and dries easily

Laundry bags: string ones with plastic zip from Woolworth's keep things separate and allow stinky socks to breathe, instead of fester

Toiletries bag with hook: for when the shower floor is grimy, hang your stuff up high

Soap dish: plastic from Boots or Superdrug

Ear plugs: noisy dogs in Nepal. Cut out the din when sharing a carriage when inter-railing

Eye sleep mask: on the equator, it gets light at 5 a.m. with sunrise at 6 a.m. Sleep in!

Survival blanket: aluminium reflects body heat for mountain trekking

Water bottle: a platypus bottle holds two litres, and compresses when empty

Torch: maglites are great for pockets – or a head torch such as petzl. Super bright LED lasts for ages.

Sunglasses: Matrix Reloaded style

Swiss Army penknife: don't leave home without one – but don't pack in hand luggage on flights

Ziplock bags: pack within your pack – sorts your clothes and keeps everything dry

Scrubbing brush: for stubborn stains! Only a good scrub on a rock in a river will do

Biodegradable liquid soap: for you and your clothes; keep the river water clean

Bath/sink plug: a sink of water, for when the river scrubbing didn't work

Washing line and pegs

Pens/journal/book to read

Camera plus film/batteries

Padlocks & chain: approx. 1.5 metres to go round backpack. Ideal when travelling on long train journeys. Stops passers-by from swiping pack from overhead racks - but don't carry in hand luggage on most flights.

Key ring personal attack alarm

Repair kit: needle, thread, buttons (for wear and tear on backpack too)

Fleece: essential for cold climates

Poncho rain mac: doubles up as a groundsheet

Loo roll/ handy pack tissues/ wet wipes: never nice being caught short

Walking boots and decent socks

Tevas/ Birkenstocks: sandals with attitude

EXTRAS

Sleeping bag/mat: not essential. Even Tibetan hostels have bed linen

Driving licence

Walkman/player

Waterproof matches

Playing cards with photos of UK on reverse: show people your home

Neck cushion: for sleeping upright on trains and planes

Binoculars

Chocolate!

WHAT NOT TO TAKE

Too much! You can always buy stuff out there

Denim: too bulky, too heavy, takes too long to dry when washed

Hairdryers: the sun can do it - or have your hair cropped so short

Medical information

Get fit! Have a pair of healthy lungs, and trek-tastic leg muscles

Immunisations: get protected with relevant jabs. Ask your GP for advice

Malaria: be warned that mefloquine (lariam) allegedly causes hallucinations and depression, and doxycycline can make skin very light-sensitive

Teeth: dental check up before you go

Eyes: Spare glasses if you wear them: if you wear contacts, talk to your optometrist about hygiene on the road and take plenty of cleaning solutions

Suntan lotion: minimum 15 SPF. Lip salve sun block. Aftersun if you forgot

Drink lots of water, a minimum of two litres a day

Wet wipes: good for wounds & face

Nail clippers: but not in hand luggage on most flights

Mosquito net

FIRST AID KIT

Any *Prescription medicines* you're on

Water purification: puritabs; or iodine droplets

Re-hydration sachets: like Dioralyte, for during/after diarrhoea

Imodium: stops the stuff from coming out on that long bus journey!

Insect repellent: deet Anthisan: contains antihistamine to treat bites

Savlon: antiseptic cream

Aspirin/paracetamol: for pain & fever

Anti motion sickness tablets

Antifungal cream

Deep Heat muscle rub

Sterile needle pack

Disposable surgical gloves

Thermometer

Scissors

Plasters, bandages & safety pins

Tweezers: get rid of ticks or splinters

Blister kit

First Aid Manual from Red Cross or St. John's Ambulance

The full version of this article, by Michelle Hawkins, was recently published in Careerscope Magazine at www. careerscope.info

Harry Hoare joined the Deloitte Scholar Programme

What are the two main things most 'gappers' what to achieve in their year? As much travelling as physically (and financially) possible along with some decent work/ job experience in a field they might like to pursue further down the line. As a Deloitte Scholar, I believe I have both.

Between September and April I am working in the Corporate Tax department of the Reading office but so far have been on numerous inductions and training events that have taken me to five-star hotels around the country, and given me an excellent grounding in the (more interesting than you would think) world of Corporate Tax, Business Skills and how to utilise a free bar whilst 'networking'. Amongst the Scholar group I have already made many good friends, some I will know at university, and plenty I hope to keep even further into the future.

Following this I have lined up some unpaid work experience in the offices of Boris Johnson MP and John Redwood MP in order to get a good understanding of how a politician's life works before reading Philosophy, Politics, and Economics at university. Study at uni will benefit from the work I'm doing now: many of the skills I have learned and I am learning will not only help me be confident when meeting new people using my improved "people skills", but also articulate my thoughts more clearly. Deloitte also provide a £1,500 travel bursary to spend in your gap year, an academic bursary of £1000 each academic year coupled with four week minimum paid work each year to ease the financial burden of student life.

Traveling-wise, I managed to squeeze 15 days in Eastern Europe into September between training courses; certainly the sights, sounds and spectacles of Prague, Budapest, Ljubljana and the rest will not soon fade from my memory. By the end of June my bank account will have had time to recover (thanks to the competitive Deloitte salary) and my dream of a round-the-world trip will be realised. Hong Kong and its inimitable hustle and bustle is the first stop before taking in Vietnam, Thailand and the surrounding area, voyaging down through Malaysia to Singapore. I can't wait to experience some of the hidden gems of the region and hit the untended trail, climbing mountains and exploring jungles.

From there I will fly to Sydney and backpack up the East coast of Australia to Cairns taking in the Aussie culture, nightlife and local beers. New Zealand is the next port of call, Christchurch and Auckland offer up most as cities but I also plan to explore some of the stunning views and landscapes seen in Lord of the Rings down in the South Island. Fiji should provide a very different atmosphere with the Cook Islands as a more chilled beach-style element that will come as welcome relaxation after packing so much in to 15 weeks. I will arrive back in England just in time for the start of the first term as a more mature and experienced person; academically, socially and personally.

Ed Frew is also on the Deloitte Scholar Programme

What did I want from a Gap year? I think the only thing I was sure about was that I didn't want to be sat at home for 15 months. I knew that if I wanted to go travelling I'd have to rustle up some funds but I didn't fancy spending 6 months on minimum wage stacking shelves at my local supermarket.

I started doing some research on the internet and, being interested in the world of business, soon picked out a number of gap year programmes in a variety of sectors. The Deloitte Scholars Scheme stood out in my eyes for a number of reasons; as well as paying you well throughout your initial 30 week placement they offered a substantial travel bursary at the end of it and then sponsorship throughout university. On top of all this there are further paid work placements – a brilliant way to top up a soon-to-be stretched student loan.

Deloitte have provided me with everything I need to do my job effectively; not just the superb top of the range laptop and mobile phone but also all-expenses paid training courses in some top-quality hotels. This meant that I could really hit the ground running when I properly started in the office. This is important as you are treated exactly the same as a new graduate. This was a huge plus for me, as was the excellent support network each new starter has, which means that there is always someone on hand if you have a problem, either with your work or otherwise.

After my placement finishes in March I will have six months to travel in. With the bursary and the money I've saved from my generous paycheques, the world will truly be my oyster. I haven't made my mind up yet as to exactly what I want to do but I do know that in eight months time I could be diving in crystal waters just off Ko Pha Ngan, bombing over the early morning powder on a fresh New Zealand piste or even driving coast to coast across the US. The decisions are the hardest bit but I'm sure I've already made the best.

Rebecca Udy discovered Italian art with Art History Abroad

I had never wanted to go to Africa. Although I could look on with admiration (and much respect) as my friends planned hikes through Nepal, teaching in Kenya or back packing across India, I knew that it was not for me. I wanted to learn, to do something cultural – to acquire knowledge not because I had to, but because I wanted to, for fun.

By the end of my exams I still had no idea what I was going to do; a term at secretarial college was planned to keep me occupied for the autumn, and very useful it was too. Yet I remained clueless about the rest of the year, until one day in September when I was surfing the gap year websites, hoping to strike lucky, and find something that did actually appeal to me. Remarkably, this is exactly what happened. As soon as I stumbled across a website advertising art history trips to Italy something inside of me leapt upwards and screamed "YES! This is it at last!". To quote their brochure, 'Art History Abroad' offered the 'opportunity to become swept up in the beauty of paintings and buildings', following in the footsteps of the 18th century Grand Tourists, who concluded from their travels, that 'Italy, its art and culture is a lifelong source of joy'. I enrolled as soon as possible.

January saw me meeting the other eighteen gap year students to begin our London week; five days going around London galleries studying Italian art. It also gave us the chance to get to know one another before spending five weeks in each others' company, and included dinner at an Italian restaurant to get us in the spirit. This was the beginning of what one of my newly-acquired friends described as six weeks of 'absolute heaven'. We wandered through Italy, beginning in Venice and moving southwards via Verona, Florence, Siena and Rome, concluding in Naples (where we climbed Vesuvius and visited the Roman remains at Herculaneum). We went on day trips to Mantua, Padua, Arezzo, Orvieto, Tivoli and Pisa. We visited churches, galleries, palaces and museums. We had long lunches in the grounds of Roman villas, and ate out nearly every night – we got pretty good at reading Italian menus!

Our tutors made the trip. They were absolutely passionate about what they taught, and went to every length possible to make it interesting and fun. It was so refreshing and exhilarating to meet people who had such a love for the arts; if we stopped in a queue, leather-bound notebooks were whipped out of their pockets, stuffed full of hand-written quotes and poetry which they read to us while we waited. We re-enacted gladiator fights in the amphitheatre in Verona, pretended to be the wealthy Medicis in their palaces in Florence and imitated sculptures by Michelangelo and Donatello.

It was freezing in Venice, and remained so in Verona and Florence, until we got further south. Our tutors could not remember it being this cold; our morning talks, if they were on architectural features or paintings in large, stone churches, had to be punctuated with thawing sessions in little cafes! We were always taught in front of the painting or building we were discussing, which made the art come alive.

One morning in Venice really stands out in my memory. We were taken to the Scuola di san Rocco, to see a whole series of paintings by Tintoretto. The light in his paintings was quite brilliant, and I saw what I think is the most beautiful depiction of the nativity I have ever seen. Through one door, stretching the entire length of the wall in front of me was the Crucifixion. I was absolutely blown away by it. It was so vivid, so full of movement, so real. My tutors had talked at the beginning of the course about the feeling you get when you come across a painting that just does it for you; when the hairs on the back of your neck stand on end, and you want to stay, forever, just drinking it in. They made up a word for it; "transcapillarytrixytremulation". I knew I had just experienced it.

We sketched, we learned, we dodged the lethal traffic and illegal handbag sellers in Florence, Verona and Siena; we even successfully got our suitcases on and off many trains and buses. Mine, I must confess was very heavy; but even I became quite adept at moving it along cobbled streets. I became best friends with the other girl who also had one of the heaviest suitcases, so we helped each other!

After the delights of Michelangelo's "David", sculptures by Donatello, the Baptistry and the Duomo in Florence, churches by Palladio, chapels by Brunelleschi and works by Giotto, Pisano, Cimabue, Ghiberti, Simone Martini, Bellini, Filippo Lippi, Fra Angelico, Pisanello, Michelozzo, Massacio, Mantegna, Botticelli, Veronese, Caravaggio, Canaletto and Tiepolo, to name but a few, we arrived in the capital city, Rome. There was much excitement amongst the group to be there at last. We were not disappointed. My first day there was spent visiting the catacombs where the Early Christians buried their dead, and one of the rooms where they used to meet, still preserved as part of a museum.

We looked out on the Pantheon from our hotel window; quite a view to wake up to in the morning! While our lunchtimes in Rome generally consisted of wonderfully lazy long picnics, where our tutors read to us about the artists, emperors, popes or poets we were studying on that day, our mornings and afternoons were packed with the delights of Rome; the fountains, the paintings, the people, the food, the ice cream.... For a prospective English undergrad, the Romantic Poets day fully lived up to expectations, as we visited Keats' house, walked the Spanish steps with Shelley and Byron, and threw flowers on Keats' grave.

For several days we thrilled to the treasures in the Vatican and Rome's museums. Then there was the Forum. We turned a corner, and there it was, lying resplendent in the brilliant Roman sunshine. Here was the real thing. Rome itself, the remnants of an empire. I will never forget the sense of awe and wonder that filled my soul at that sight. It truly was magnificent. We could even trace the cart wheel ruts in the paving stones with our toes! On our last night in Rome, after a delicious meal where for once I don't think I ate pasta, we climbed to see the Forum by moonlight. It was magical. After a long night of dancing and bidding a fond farewell to such a glorious city, we left for Naples.

Naples was poorer, and probably truer to real Italy, as there were fewer tourists, food was simpler and cheaper, and you had to watch out for fast handbag-snatching motorbikes zipping past your shoulders. No more of the expensive shops and the well dressed shoppers that accompanied them. I managed to get ill on our last night in Italy; my friend bathed my forehead to get my temperature down while she got ready for supper! I made it out to our final meal, however, and improved as the evening progressed. I was so glad not to miss our farewell speeches over dinner, and the last night of fun with the lovable bunch I had grown so attached to. We have just had a reunion, and are all unanimous that we want to go back and do it all over again.

I see the trip as a rite of passage; a fundamental part of my education. I returned wiser, and feel much more confident going into an arts degree with such an understanding and a love for the arts behind me. I have also made friends I will keep for life. The experience was unforgettable. I LOVED it.

Jenny Campbell, a GAP Activity Projects placement in Tanzania

I decided to take a gap year for a number of reasons. Firstly I wanted to see new places and have a chance to broaden my horizons, but I didn't want to spend the year just travelling, I wanted to do something useful with my time. I also thought that taking a year off between school and university would give me a chance to form a clearer idea of what I wanted to study and what career I wanted to pursue.

My GAP placement was at Kilombero Sugar Company, Tanzania. I knew I would like to go to a country in Africa, and that I would like to work with children. The GAP team were very helpful in suggesting places for me to go and in the end we decided that this one was most suited to what I wanted to do and so I spent the year at Kilombero teaching in a primary school, running a kids club, setting up a library and running some adult English classes.

It's difficult to pick out the best parts of my placement because I had such an amazing time. However, one of my favourite parts was singing with the children. The kids had so much energy and enthusiasm and lessons were just so much fun. The kids can now even entertain with their own versions of "We Will Rock You" and "We Are The Champions".

I travelled both within school holidays and after my placement had finished. During the school holidays we climbed Mount Kilimanjaro – and made it to the top!! We went on a safari, and spent Christmas on Zanzibar. After my placement I travelled through further parts of Tanzania, through Zambia to Victoria Falls, where I completed the Victoria Falls 111m bungy jump and then travelled in Malawi before returning back to Tanzania.

You go away as a group of people not knowing much about each other only having met a few times before, and come home with some of the best friends you will ever make. You also get the chance to meet people from all over the world who are travelling or working in the country of your placement.

Having done a GAP placement and having spent some time travelling, I would highly recommend a GAP placement for anyone taking a year out. The placement provides you with a chance to actually live in a country and become a part of it, rather than just being someone who is passing through. It also gives you a chance to do something useful with your time, and contribute something back to the country.

Travelling is lots of fun, but if you have the chance to take a GAP placement I would highly recommend it as it is a really rewarding experience which I'm very glad I did.

Evan Bailey trained as a snowboard instructor with Peak Leaders

I decided to train as a snowboard Instructor when I first went to the snow in Victoria, Australia in 1998. I had an amazing time riding with my friends and although the conditions were average I knew snowboarding was for me!! Since then I've been hooked and having a chance to work doing something you love is fantastic. I didn't see it as a job at all, just a great lifestyle and a ticket to travel!

Peak Leaders made the amazing training we had 6 days a week on an average of 5 hours a day so interesting - I don't know if I would call it training as I expected it to be! It was definitely one of the best experiences of my life - 9 weeks riding with mates while improving my skills with awesome instructors and riders! Canada was magic, and everyday seemed better than the last. Memories that will last forever.

The experience of training was so beneficial. Personally I learnt to set achievable goals to work towards - not only Instructor qualifications but physically being fitter and more flexible. My passion for snowboarding helped me work toward these goals and stay focused, giving 100%!

There is nothing better than having a job you love! So if skiing or boarding is your thing, do it! Peak Leaders provided the perfect opportunity to get stacks of qualifications and the 9 weeks was my most memorable ever! Not only through riding perfect champagne powder or improving 100%, but riding with mates you keep for life sharing the same passion as you. Those are the memories you won't forget!

Damien Rickwood, on a Trekforce placement in Central American

I chose to do a Trekforce placement in Central America because it offered a combination of activities. I spent two months on a project building a ranger station in the jungle, one month learning Spanish in Guatemala and two months teaching in a community school. I wanted to spend a significant amount of time away in order to get a real feel for the culture of the country and five months seemed just right.

To raise the money to go I had a full time job but I also held a barbeque, a raffle and received sponsorship from my school. I raised £1500 through fundraising. I found the fundraising really difficult but if I did it again I would definitely try to fundraise more of the money.

From doing my gap year with Trekforce I learnt that there is so much to see and do out there and an organised expedition is possibly the best way to see it all and you get opportunities that individual travelers miss out on. I also learnt so much about the cultures of Belize and Guatemala without really realising it, instead I lived it!

The best moment of my project was the opening ceremony of project because it was such a massive sense of achievement. It was opened by the directors of a local conservation charity and they had big plans to continue developing the site for research and eco-tourism etc. It was brilliant to know that what we had slaved on for 2 months was just the beginning of bigger things. Other high points were reaching the destination of our 5 day trek through the Cockscomb Basin Jaguar Reserve and simple things such as gazing up at the stars on a full belly of Spam and noodles and making some brilliant friends.

The teaching phase was really challenging - mainly because of the culture differences. My teaching partner and I were placed in a remote Maya village in the south of Belize. One of the most difficult things was to have people staring at you wherever you go. But eventually you feel like you really belong. This was what I feel was my biggest achievement whilst teaching; becoming part of the family I was living with.

As for moments that I will always remember, we helped the school enter an Arts Festival and seeing all of our kids performing on stage was really exciting. We were so proud of them!

There were a few bad moments on project, mostly to do with the really hard work we did! Now I look back and think it was just character building. The jungle trek I did was the hardest thing I have done in my life also the biggest adventure.

Rachel Smith, conservation and teaching in Borneo with Trekforce

During my gap year I wanted to see a different culture but also wanted to do something that contributed to the country I visited. I really wanted to challenge myself by doing something completely different and adventurous and the charity Trekforce Expeditions was recommended to me by a friend.

I spent two months living and working in the rainforest within the beautiful Maliau Basin with a team of 20 other volunteers (plus expedition leaders and medics). We built a scientific studies centre which will help prevent the Basin from being logged in the future. I also went on a trek which was tough but incredibly rewarding – we saw amazing jungle and waterfalls and lots of wildlife – monkeys, orang-utans, crocodiles and hornbills to name a few! Barely anyone is allowed into the Basin so it was a unique experience that I wouldn't have got just backpacking.

I then went on to teach (with another volunteer) in a remote Kelabit school for a further two months. The kids in my class were brilliant – really lively and sometimes difficult to control - but so enthusiastic to learn. I lived with a wonderful family who treated us like their own family. I was so sad when the time came to leave but I think my time in Borneo were the best months of my life!

Iain Walters joined VentureCo's Aztec-Maya Venture

Taking a Gap Year is a pretty serious decision. There are several basic things you should establish; Will I do something worthwhile? Can I afford it? Will I be able to go to the university of my choice? The things that universities like to see (and which are a lot of fun) are travelling to somewhere new, doing charity work, learning a language and doing something related to your course.

I went away with a company called VentureCo to Central America. I chose them because they were pretty much all inclusive, so I knew where I was with my money before I went. They also offered some pretty amazing experiences like cycling around Cuba and climbing the highest peak in Central America, not to mention living in the jungle for a month doing conservation work.

A three week language school was also included and trust me, this is a must for any traveller (talking to the locals makes your trip so much better). We visited quite a lot of Mayan ruins during the trip, and as I am now studying History it was great to do something related to my course. The money side was hard, travelling isn't always cheap so make sure you go away knowing how much things are going to cost! It's a good idea to make sure you have a job before you start your Gap year so that you know how much you can spend!

My Gap year was incredible. The people I met and the experiences I had were unforgettable. I would definitely recommend it to anyone but make sure you do something extraordinary with the time. After all, these are the best years of your life!

Dan Heymann experiences VentureCo's Himalaya 4 expedition

Nothing can really prepare a person for his first visit to Delhi. In our case, a mammoth journey taking in two stopovers with only the pictures from 'The Italian Job' as preparation. Despite this, we were all excited to have finally arrived: our first few days certainly gave us lots of interesting experiences. I don't think any of us will ever again complain about the driving back home after having been in a rickshaw that swerved violently to miss a cow that has suddenly decided to sit in the middle of the road. Similarly, no English pub can ever quite match the atmosphere of 'Blues' where we were served by Indians dressed as cowboys! Cowboys and 'Indians' takes on a whole new context!

After a few days to meet the new culture we were ready to move on. This gave us our first experience of the Indian railway network: coming from England it is difficult to criticise other countries rail systems. Difficult, but not impossible! Delhi railway station is in a league of its own. Notice boards change train platforms with routine regularity, food sellers think nothing of reheating food that they have dropped on the floor and at no other railway station have I played a game of 'guess how much poo will be left on the tracks once the train leaves'. Inside the train, the world becomes even madder, as we argued with old ladies who refused to give up the seats that we were supposed to be in. It was like a journey out of a Michael Palin travel TV programme, except that we all got to experience it rather than watch it!

The fruits of our effort was that we got to the beautiful city of Rishikesh, high in the Indian Himalaya, on the banks of the Ganges with narrow atmospheric streets that are traffic free, meaning that you only have to avoid the cows, which everyone apart from Faye seemed capable of doing. Our mornings were spent on the rooftop overlooking the mountains doing yoga sessions. We quickly came to realise that when our instructor told us only to push our body as far as was comfortable, this really meant that once we had reached our pain barrier, he would come and push us a little bit further! All in the cause of Reiki! Afternoons were taken up with all sorts of lessons: Hindi, meditation, and cookery all featured, though no-one took up the body love stretching lessons advertised at the German bakery. The brave and uninhibited amongst us even had a massage.

After all this pampering, we were ready to set off for our preparatory trek in the Himalayas. The trail stretched us all as we were climbing over 1000m with all our kit with us. Yet the sense of achievement at the end of the day, as well as the stunning views made it worthwhile. And every evening once we'd set up our campsite, our pains were forgotten as we sat around Rob's 'no match' campfire, drinking Herculean amounts of garam chai and listening to the songs and stories of our favourite photoguide and guru of all things outdoor Chowhain. We even managed to pick up an extra member of the group for part of our travels, a friendly dog who followed us, affectionately known by all the group as Spadger.

The outdoors adventure came to a close with a 2 day rafting trip down the Ganges. At times, it felt a bit like being in a washing machine on spin, but then you would splash out onto flat water and pass pilgrims bathing, or fall in yourself and have to wait to be flushed out of the Holy water, and you knew that you could only be in India.

So now, a little browner and much fitter, we head off to Kathmandu, to see whether Simon's friends really do exist and to start off on the trek to Everest.

This section includes a number of organisations which offer gap year planning services, safety awareness training, security advice and health care information through intensive courses and briefing sessions or web-based services.

Association of British Travel Agents

68-71 Newman St., London W1T 3AH
Tel: 020 7637 2444   Fax: 020 7637 0713
Email: information@abta.co.uk   Web: www.abta.com

ABTA is main trade association for UK tour operators and travel agents, and a number of the travel organisations included in this directory are ABTA-bonded companies. The ABTA Information Department offers advice on travel related subjects and can verify the ABTA membership of any operator. Travel information telephone helpline is provided on 0901 201 5050 (UK callers only), but calls to this service are charged at an additional rate.

Adventure Activities Licensing Authority

17 Lambourne Crescent, Llanishen, Cardiff CF14 5GS
Tel: 02920 755715
Web at www.aala.org

AALA is an independent, cross-departmental public authority, funded by the Department of Education and Skills, and operating under the written guidance of the Health and Safety Commission. In effect it is an independent watchdog on the delivery of outdoor adventure activities for young people. Both consumers and those thinking of working in this area would be well advised to check the position of any organisation to which they are considering applying.

Association of Independent Tour Operators (AITO)

133A St Margaret's Road, Twickenham, Middlesex TW1 1RG
Tel: 020 8744 9280   Fax: 020 8744 3187
Email: info@aito.co.uk   Web: www.aito.co.uk

This organisation represents around 160 of Britain's specialist tour operators. AITO members are vetted and fully bonded for clients' protection, in compliance with UK and European regulations. AITO members are required to protect money paid by customers to the member for any holiday sold under the AITO logo and to comply with UK Government Regulations in this respect.

Association of Language Travel Organisations

Bredgade 25H, DK-1260, Copenhagen K Denmark
Tel: (+45) 3317 0062   Fax (+45) 3393 9676
Email: mailbox@altonet.org   Web: www.altonet.org

Formed in 1998, ALTO has grown to an association of buyers and sellers of language travel programmes and national language travel associations. It works to protect the clients of ALTO members - 185 language schools, travel agents and associations working in 43 countries. All ALTO members agree to adhere to the ALTO Charter and Guarantees of Quality. The website includes a list of members.

British Activity Holiday Association

22 Green Lane, Hersham, Walton on Thames KT12 5HD
Tel: 01932 252994   **Fax: 01932 252994**
Email: info@baha.org.uk   **Web: www.baha.org.uk**

The trade association for private sector providers of activity holidays and courses in the UK. Member centres abide by the BAHA Code of Practice. The web site includes information about the BAHA Quality Assurance Statement, a summary of BAHA Safety Standards and a consumer guide for anyone seeking an activity holiday in the UK or abroad.

Careerscope Travel Jouornal

www.csjournal.co.uk

Our web-based travel journal service provide an area on the internet exclusively for travellers to record their trip and keep in touch with friends and family. Show everyone what a great time you're having. In return for a small subscription, users have a unique web address, exclusively for their personal journal entries and photographs, plus a personal message board that friends can use to keep in touch.

Caroline's Rainbow Foundation

PO Box 216, York YO42 4WZ
Tel: 01759 304425   **Fax: 01759 304425**
Email: contact@carolinesrainbowfoundation.org
Web: www.carolinesrainbowfoundation.com

Marjorie Marks-Stuttle, her son Richard and husband David Marks have established Caroline's Rainbow Foundation, a charity formed after the tragic death of her daughter Caroline in 2002 in Bundaberg, Australia whilst backpacking in her gap year.

The aims of the charity are to help fund backpackers in Australia, and ultimately the backpacking "route", if they find themselves in distress or financial hardship. One-day seminars, providing advice and guidance for parents, teachers and young travellers planning a gap year, are organised.

This new charity welcomes donations and support.

Davies Laing and Dick

10 Pembridge Square, London W2 4ED
Tel: 020 7727 2797   Fax: 020 7792 0730
Email: dld@dld.org   Web: www.dld.org

The college runs a number of courses for pre-university students. Students can retake A levels or even start a new A level from scratch. Careers and UCAS advice is offered to all students. There is a high-powered Oxbridge Entrance Course which includes philosophy, current affairs, degree subject tuition, interview technique and practice. Pre-foundation art portfolio courses include fine art, ceramics, graphics, photography, textiles and sculpture. In addition to the conventional school subjects DLD offers film and media studies, music technology, psychology and philosophy. At least one pre-university student each year helps with secretarial and reception duties.

Department of Health Advice for Travellers

Web: www.dh.gov.uk (Select Travellers' Health from the home page)

Essential advice for travellers about planning ahead, staying healthy and getting treatment elsewhere in the world - plus information about the E111 'passport' to free or reduced-cost emergency care in most other European countries.

Federation of International Youth Travel Organisations

Bredgade 25H, 1260 Copenhagen K, Denmark
Tel: (+45) 3333 9600   Fax: (+45) 3393 9676
Email: mailbox@fiyto.org   Web: www.fiyto.org

FIYTO has 450 member organisations from over 70 countries representing the international youth travel industry. Members are required to follow a strict code of ethical standards. The website includes a list of members.

Foreign and Commonwealth Office

King Charles Street, London SW1A 2AH
Tel: 0870 606 0290   Web: www.fco.gov.uk

The Foreign & Commonwealth Office works for UK interests throughout the world, with some 16,000 satff based in the UK and in the overseas network of over 200 diplomatic offices. The FCO Travel Advice Unit aims to ensure that British travellers are well prepared before departure. The website includes extensive travel advice, including lists of regions where the FCO advises against travel, detailed travellers' tips' and information about UK embassies and representation throughout the world.

Gabbitas Educational Consultants

Carrington House, 126-130 Regent Street, London W1B 5EE
Tel: 020 7734 0161   Fax: 020 7437 1764
Web:www.gabbitas.co.uk

Gabbitas provides a range of advisory services for parents and students at all stages of education. Their consultants have a wide knowledge of independent schools and colleges throughout the UK, including sixth-form and vocational colleges, and can also advise on opportunities for language study and other courses abroad. The School Selection Service offers personal, expert advice on the choice of an independent school or college. It can be particularly helpful for school-leavers and students who wish to retake A levels or to change school at 16.

There is no charge to the parent or students for this service. The Consultancy Service, for which a fee is charged, enables clients to discuss any educational matter in depth with an experienced consultant. For students aged 15 plus, this includes education and training options at 16, choice of degree courses and universities, UCAS applications, gap year options, job applications and interview techniques.

Gap Enterprise

East Manor Barn, Fringford, Oxfordshire OX27 8DG.
Tel: 01869 278346 Fax: 01869 278097
Email: johnvessey@gapenterprise.co.uk   Web: www.gapenterprise.co.uk

Gap Enterprise is an independent gap year consultancy which aims to encourage gappers to enjoy themselves while drawing on the full potential of those valuable fifteen months between school and university. We inform, inspire, motivate and help structure gaps, while providing all the essentials for a young person to organise their own programme. The impartial service is delivered through private consultation and comprehensive written report.

International Society of Travel Medicine

PO Box 871089, Stone Mountain, Georgia 30087-0028 USA
Tel: (+1) 770 736 7060   Fax: (+1) 770 736 6732
Email: istm@istm.org   Web: www.istm.org

The ISTM website includes a worldwide travel clinic directory.

The Knowledge Gap

Pitt Farmhouse, Chevithorne, Devon EX16 7PU
Tel: 01884 258724
Email: info@kgap.co.uk   Web: www.kgap.co.uk

The Knowledge Gap was established in 2001 by three former HM Special Forces soldiers who identified a demand amongst school leavers for gaining some practical advice on travel safety prior to embarking on their gap year. Advice is provided through a three-day residential course based on Exmoor where students stay in youth hostel accommodation and receive a mixture of indoor and outdoor instruction from both in-house staff, paramedics, firefighters, police officers and lifeboatmen.

LocateU

178 Urban Road, Hexthorpe, Doncaster DN4 0EZ
Tel: 01302 561079
Email: via website   Web: www.locateu.co.uk

This organisation offers a subscription service that will allow gap year travellers to log on to a central system so that someone knows where they have gone, when they are due back and if needs must what medical conditions they may have.

MASTA (Medical Advisory Services for Travellers Abroad)

Moorfield Road, Yeadon, Leeds, West Yorkshire LS19 7BN
Tel: 0113 238 7500
Web: www.masta.org and www.masta.info

MASTA was set up in 1984 at the London School of Hygiene and Tropical Medicine with the aim of raising awareness of health issues associated with travel. Services range from the supply of vaccines and travel medicines to research on important travel issues.

Objective Travel Safety Ltd

Bragborough Lodge Farm, Braunston, Daventry, Northants NN11 7HA
Tel: 01788 899029
Email: office@objectiveteam.com   Web: www.objectivegapsafety.com

Specialists in training journalists and industry professionals operating in war zones, Objective Team has developed a Gap Safety course. In one day, students are given advice, warnings and responses to various situations they may face. The course covers security advice, what to take, safe food and water, accommodation security, medical and extreme situations.

Red24

Tel: 0207 332 5618   Fax: 0208 707 0002
Email: red24@red24.info   Web: www.red24.info

Red24 is a membership organisation which provides access to 24-hour security advice by an interactive website, phone, fax and e-mail. advice is offered at two levels: rreventative advice - providing tailored advice for the avoidance of risk, e.g. the planning of gap years and trips abroad; reactive advice - online advice, 24 hours per day, 7 days a week, when confronted with risk or threat, e.g. theft, stalking, arrest, kidnapping.

Safetrek

East Culme House, Cullompton, Devon EX15 1NX
Tel: 01884 839704
Email: info@safetrek.co.uk   Web: wwwsafetrek.co.uk

Safetrek delivers safety awareness and personal security training for young travellers both at home and abroad. One course is specifically designed for young adults contemplating travelling abroad on the their GAP year. By the end of the course they will have the confidence, knowledge and awareness to deal with problems associated with travelling (pick-pocketing, loss of documents, first aid) to the much more serious (robbery and rape) and resolve them successfully.

The second course is designed for those about to embark on a University course. Statistically people living in UK are more at risk than those travelling abroad especially in big cities. By the end of this course they will understand how to be situationally aware and protect themselves from burglaries, harassment, robbery and rape.

The Suzy Lamplugh Trust

PO Box 17818, London SW14 8WW
Tel: 0208 876 0305   Fax: 0208 876 0891
Email: info@suzylamplugh.org   Web: www.suzylamplugh.org

This registered charity is the leading authority on personal safety. The Trust works alongside government, the police, the educational establishment, public bodies and the business sector to encourage safety wherever people may be at risk. As well as being dedicated to improving personal safety for all, whether female or male, young or old, the Trust undertakes a wide range of research, campaigning, training, education and practical support activities to put its aims into practice. The Trust's network of registered Trust Trainers provide tailored in-house courses for a diverse range of organisations, including schools and colleges. The Trust's nation-wide register of accredited Personal Safety at Work Trainers includes a number who also act as consultants.

United States Center for Disease Control and Prevention

Web: www.cdc.gov/travel

The US Department of Health and Human Services (Center for Disease Control and Prevention) provides this very detailed website with information on a wide range of international travel health issues

- including vaccinations, insect and arthropod protection, safe food and water, travel medicine clinics (US and international) and information for special needs travellers.

Year Out Group

Queensfield, 28 Kings Road, Easterton, Wiltshire SN10 4PX
Tel: 07980 395789
Email: info@yearoutgroup.org   **Web: www.yearoutgroup.org**

The Year Out Group is an association of leading year out organisations that was formed in 1998 to promote the concept and benefits of well-structured year out programmes, to promote models of good practice and to help young people and their advisers in selecting suitable and worthwhile projects. Members of the Year Out Group agree to adhere to the Code of Practice - full details on the website.

Peak Leaders

BTCV

African Conservation Experience

Raleigh International

Eco Africa Experience

Venture Co

African Conservation Experience

BTCV

British Institute in Florence

eaching & Projects Abroad

Raleigh International

Venture Co

Vitalise

Madventurer

Trekforce

World Challenge Expeditions

Madventurer

Peak Leaders

GAP Activity Projects

British Institute in Florence

Trekforce

Raleigh International

Venture Co

BSES Expeditions

This section combines information about a selection of voluntary and paid work opportunities throughout the UK. Some of the organisations offer specific gap year programmes; others welcome gap year students alongside other voilunteers. A local volunteer bureau may also have information about a range of opportunities in a particular area. Many international aid organisations also offer UK-based work opportunities, such as head office administration and fundraising activities.

Community programmes

AFS Youth Development

Leeming House, Vicar Lane, Leeds LE2 7JF
Tel: 0113 2426136   Web: 0113 2430631
Email: info-unitedkingdom@afs.org   Web: www.afsuk.org

AFS is an international, voluntary, non-governmental, not-for-profit organization that provides intercultural learning opportunities to help people develop the knowledge, skills and understanding needed to create a more just and peaceful world. From its origins in the American Field Service ambulance, AFS has become committed to contributing to international understanding through exchanges. There are many opportunities of volunteers throughout the UK.

Age Concern

Astral House, 1268 London Road, London SW16 4ER
Tel: 020 8765 7200   Fax: 020 8765 7240
Email: enquiries@ageconcern.org.uk   Web: www.ageconcern.org.uk

Local Age Concerns provide services which enable older people to continue to live independently and make the most of life. Many of these local services just wouldn't happen without the help of people like you. As a volunteer, you could be doing anything from driving a minibus to running an exercise class – so whether you have a lot of time to give or just a little, and whatever your interests, we've probably got a volunteering opportunity to suit you.

L'Arche

10 Briggate, Silsden, Keighley, West Yorkshire BD20 9JT
Tel: 01535 656186   Fax: 01535 656426
Email: info@larch.org.uk   Web: www.larche.org.uk

L'Arche Communities are places where people are valued not for what they have or can do but for who they are as a person. L'Arche believes everyone has a unique value and the same dignity and rights, whatever their gifts and limitations. L'Arche enables people with learning disabilities and their assistants to live and work very much as family and friends rather than clients and staff. Through the relationships formed within L'Arche houses and workshops and the wider community, people with learning disabilities are helped to grow in trust and confidence towards greater independence of spirit and, where possible, of self-care. Centred in Bognor Regis, Brecon, Kent, Edinburgh, Inverness, Liverpool, London and Preston. L'Arche UK Communities form part of a world-wide federation founded by Jean Vanier. Assistants receive in-service training, free board and lodging and pocket money. No qualifications are needed, though craft and domestic skills are useful. Although Christian in practice, L'Arche welcomes people from other faiths or none.

Most Communities look for a minimum commitment of 12 months. Contact John Peet, General Secretary, at the above address for further information and an application form. A registered charity.

Braendam Family House

Braendam, Thornhill, Stirling FK8 3QH
Tel:01786 850259   **Fax:01786 850738**
Email: info@braendam.org.uk   **Web: www.braendam.org.uk**

For over 30 years Braendam Family House has provided respite for families living in poverty, and encountering deprivation, ill health and adverse circumstances. The volunteers' role is to support the families on their holiday. They need to be able to listen and talk to them in a positive, non-judgemental way, accompanying them on trips; play with children and adults; organise games etc; encourage participation and raise environmental awareness. They also help with domestic duties. Their time is split between spending time with families and maintaining the house to a high domestic standard – to come in line with Care legislation.

There are places for six volunteers for a minimum of six months to a year. A year gives volunteers maximum benefit. The first month is a 'no-strings' trial on both sides. A couple of extra volunteers are employed in the summer holidays, at Christmas and during a two week winter work camp.Volunteers receive full board, weekly pocket money and a contribution towards travelling costs. These are demanding positions, but training, support and supervision are provided. This is an excellent opportunity for a rewarding and valuable experience of working with people. Volunteers should preferably be aged over 21, but younger applicants may be considered. Driving licence very useful.

British Red Cross

9 Grosvenor Crescent, London SW1X 7EJ
Tel: 020 7201 5142
Email: local contacts via website   Web site: www.redcross.org.uk

The British Red Cross cares for people in crisis in local communities throughout the UK and overseas as part of the International Red Cross and Red Crescent Movement - assisting in the aftermath of natural and made disasters. There are local volunteer opportunities for a whole range of activities with the British Red Cross, depending on your interests. There are also volunteer opportunities at the London head office.

Camphill Communities

Co-worker Development Office, 55 Cainscross Road, Stroud GL5 4EX
Tel: 01453 753142   Fax: 01453 767469
Email: coworker@camphill.org.uk   Web: www.camphill.org.uk

A Camphill community is created by a group of people who live, learn and work together according to Christian ideals and deriving inspiration from the philosophy of Rudolf Steiner. The co-workers, and those with special needs who come to communities, live together in an atmosphere of mutual respect. There are 47 communities are in the UK and Ireland, plus a further 40 communities around the world.

CARE (Cottage and Rural Enterprises Ltd)

9 Weir Road, Kibworth, Leicester LE8 0QL
Tel: 0116 279 3225   Fax: 0116 279 6384
Email: carecentral@freeuk.com   Web: www.care-ltd.co.uk

This organisation was founded with the aim of providing residential and day care facilities for people with a learning disability, promoting an active and stimulating lifestyle. Young people with drive and the ability to relate to residents are needed to work in communities throughout England. Minimum six weeks all year round. Food, accommodation and weekly payment provided. Regional locations are in Devon, Kent, Lancashire, Leicestershire, Newcastle-upon-Tyne, Shropshire, Wiltshire, West Sussex.

ChildHope UK

Lector Court, 151 Farringdon Road, London EC1R 3AF
Tel: 020 7833 0868   Fax: 020 7833 2500
Email: chuk@gn.apc.org   Website: www.childhopeuk.org

The organisation is dedicated to improving the lives and defending the rights of street children worldwide through the development of appropriate practice, project partnership, capacity building, support and advocacy. UK volunteering opportunities may include fundraising administration and research, general administration and translation.

Christian Aid

35 Lower Marsh, London SE1 7RL
Tel: 020 7620 4444   **Fax: 020 7620 0719**
Email: info@christian-aid.org   **Web: www.christian-aid.org.uk**

Gap year scheme: Join one of our area teams in the UK and spend a year getting young people fired up about poverty and injustice, through events, workshops, worship and campaigns. A scheme fee is payable, but members receive accommodation, food and a weekly allowance. Internship scheme: Christian Aid also runs an internship scheme. This is mainly office-based work in London. A salary is paid, but participants are responsible for all their own living and accommodation costs.

CSV

237 Pentonville Road, London N1 9NJ
Tel: Volunteer Freephone 0800 374991
Email: volunteer@csv.org.uk   **Web: www.csv.org.uk**

UK charity CSV offers you the chance to do something positive in a gap year, whatever your grades. If you are aged over 16 with 4 to 12 months to spare (3 month summer placements are available) CSV can place you where your help is needed on one of hundreds of voluntary projects throughout Britain. For example, you could help homeless people in a hostel, support young people leaving care, assist students with disabilities at university, enable carers to have a break or mentor young offenders. No previous experience or specific qualifications are needed; training and support given. Placements are guaranteed for everyone willing to work full-time and away from home. Each of our several thousands of volunteers receives free accommodation, travel expenses, food and a weekly allowance. With CSV you will gain skills and experience that look good on your UCAS form or CV. Apply at any time to start at any time.

Corrymeela Community

Corrymeela Centre, Ballycastle, Co. Antrim BT54 6QU
Tel:02820 762626
Email:ballycastle@corrymeela.org   **Web: www.corrymeela.org**

The Corrymeela Community is an ecumenical Christian organisation committed to reconciliation in Ireland and throughout the world. Approximately 16 volunteers are needed each July-August to work in the following areas: arts & crafts; recreation; family/group helper; housekeeping; kitchen; music; worship. Application forms available early in the year - deadline 1 April. Also 12 long term (6 months/1 year) volunteers with varied responsibilities. Approx. half from outside Ireland. Minimum age 18. Hours: flexible, but generally long. Stamina and humour a must. Applicants need not be Christian, but open to people from all backgrounds and willing to support Corrymeela's Christian ethos. 1 year begins September, apply by 1 March. 6 months begins March, apply by 1 December. All volunteers receive free board/lodgings; long-term volunteers also receive a weekly stipend. For information write to Volunteer Coordinator.

do-it.org.uk

Web: www.do-it.org.uk

An online database for UK volunteering opportunities which can be searched by town and activity. The site also includes other useful information about volunteering.

Girlguiding UK

17-19 Buckingham Palace Road, London SW1W OPT
Tel: 020 7834 6242　　　　　Fax: 020 7630 6199
Email:chq@girlguiding.org.uk　　Web: www.girlguiding.org.uk

Membership of Guiding is essential. Work usually consists of a variety of practical and administrative duties with Training and Activity Centres both in the UK and abroad. The Association also runs a scheme whereby members can become involved in overseas community development projects. Projects can involve any of the following activities and are normally two to four weeks in duration: primary health care, conservation and ecology schemes, teaching English as a Foreign Language, training of leaders, promotion of Guiding and Guiding Development.

Independent Living Alternatives

Trafalgar House, Grenville Place, London NW7 3SA
Tel: 020 8906 9265　　　　　Fax: 020 8906 9265
Email: enquiry@ILAnet.co.uk　　Web: www.ILAnet.co.uk

ILA is a registered charity which recruits volunteers in London and Cumbria to help disabled people live independently. Volunteers with ILA receive free accommodation, ongoing training, support and supervision, living expenses and regular time off. No experience is necessary.

The Leonard Cheshire Foundation

30 Millbank, London SW1P 4QD
Tel: 020 7802 8200　　　　　Fax: 020 7802 8250
Email: volunteers@lc-uk.org　Web: www.leonard-cheshire.org.uk

Leonard Cheshire is the UK's leading voluntary sector provider of support services for disabled people. We support 21,000 disabled people in the UK, offering flexible services to meet a wide range of needs, which include: care at home services; care homes with and without nursing, including respite care; day services including resource centres; independent / supported living units; acquired brain injury rehabilitation services; recreational services and education, training and employment support through Workability and jobability.com. Leonard Cheshire also campaigns for the rights of disabled people in the UK and raises awareness of the issues affecting them. We also work with disabled people in 57 countries worldwide working in partnership with more than 255 locally run and managed services and organisations. Volunteers play an important role in our work with disabled people and can make a real difference to people's lives.

The role of overseas volunteers is to enhance the lives of the people who use our residential services by supporting them to take part in activities, whether inside the home, or in the community. Volunteers work in conjunction with the paid staff and, with the agreement of the volunteer and the disabled person, volunteers may be asked to assist with personal care tasks during busy times, such as at meal times or on excursions. Volunteers must be over 18 years old and are provided with accommodation, meals, a weekly allowance, and appropriate training. The minimum period is 6 months and applicants are accepted through the following agencies: GAP, CET or ICYE-UK, please contact Leonard Cheshire for more information.

Mencap

123 Golden Lane, London EC1Y 0RT
Tel: 020 7454 0454   **Fax: 020 7696 5540**
Email: information@mencap.org.uk   **Web: www.mencap.org.uk**

Mencap works with people with a learning disability and their families and carers. It campaigns to ensure that their rights are recognised and that they are respected as individuals, and provides support with housing, education, employment and leisure activities. The organisation relies on thousands of volunteers to support many of its activities and services.

Millennium Volunteers

Department for Education and Skills, E4C, Moorfoot, Sheffield S1 4PQ
Email: millennium.volunteers@dfes.gsi.gov.uk
Web: www.millenniumvolunteers.gov.uk

Millennium Volunteers, aged between 16 and 24, give up free time to help their local communities. You might find them coaching a school football team, working at a community radio station or helping create a garden for local residents. MV allows young people to build on their interests, to develop themselves and make a difference to their community at the same time.

Over142,000 young people have joined the MV programme, with over 70,000 achieving 100 hour awards and over 49,000 achieving the 200 hour Award of Excellence for Volunteering.

The Mission to Seafarers

St Michael Paternoster Royal, College Hill, London EC4R 2RL
Tel: 020 7248 5202   Fax: 020 7248 4761
Email: ministry@missiontoseafarers.org   Web: www.missiontoseafarers.org

Candidates aged 21 to 26, Christian, can be accepted for one year helping to run clubs and recreational facilities, ship and hospital visiting, and assisting the Chaplain. The gap year scheme is open to those looking to gain wider experience through service to others before taking up work or furthering their education. It may be of particular interest to those who are thinking of full-time ministry in the church and who want to undertake a practical Christian mission.

UK ports where chaplain's assistants have been placed in recent years include Liverpool and Southampton. Candidates should have a valid driving licence. Travel costs, board and lodging and pocket money provided. Contact the Ministry Secretary. There are also opportunities to work in international ports (see entry the following section).

Ockenden International

Constitution Hill, Woking, Surrey, GU22 7UU
Tel: 01483 772012   Fax: 01483 750774
Email: oi@ockenden.org.uk   Web: www.ockenden.org.uk

Ockenden operates in some of the poorest countries of Africa and Asia, working with people who have been displaced from their homes through war, famine or drought. Ockenden has UK volunteer opportunities for people wanting to help fundraise in local communities. There are occasional opportunities at the Woking head office, mainly in office hours. Some internships of 3-6 months are also available . Interns would normally receive travel and lunch money. Areas may include policy, media, publications and others.

Oxfam

274 Banbury Rd, Oxford OX2 7DZ
Tel: 0870 333 2700
Email: givetime@oxfam.org.uk   Web: www.oxfam.org.uk

Oxfam has an on going requirement for volunteers at its head office in Oxford, and in regional offices in London, Bristol, Cardiff, Birmingham, Newcastle, Manchester and Glasgow. Sometimes a post may require a specialist skill, sometimes it may need someone who simply has a great deal of enthusiasm.

It may be a full time post over some months or it may be short term and part time. The UK network of 700 shops provides further volunteer opportunities. A volunteer application form can be downloaded from the website.

Pax Christi

Christian Peace Educaton Centre, St. Joseph's, Watford Way, Hendon, London NW4 4TY
Tel: 020 8203 4884   **Fax: 020 8203 5234**
Email: paxchristi@gn.apc.org   **Web: www.paxchristi.org.uk**

An international Christian movement promoting peace through an active role in the community. Takes energetic and active volunteers to work at a youth hostel in London and to staff playschemes in Northern Ireland for three to five weeks in July and August. Free time activities organised. Minimum age 19.

The Prince's Trust Volunteers Programme

18 Park Square East, London NW1 4LH
Tel: 020 7543 1234   **Fax: 020 7543 1200**
Email: info@princes-trust.org.uk   **Web: www.princes-trust.org.uk**

The Prince's Trust is the UK's leading youth charity offering 14 to 30 year olds opportunities to develop confidence, learn new skills, get into work and start businesses. The Trust targets people who are unemployed or facing barriers in life. The Prince's Trust Volunteers Programme was launched in 1990.

This award-winning programme enables employed and unemployed 16 to 25 year olds to work together to develop their confidence, motivation and skills through teamwork in the community. The programme sets up teams of up to 15 people. Each team is led by a trained leader on a series of team-building activities including individual placements, group projects and an outdoor residential week

Quaker Voluntary Action

Friends Meeting House, 6 Mount Street, Manchester M2 5NS
Tel: 0845 456 0353   **Fax; 0161 819 1634**
Email: mail@qva.org.uk   **Web: www.qva.org.uk**

QVA runs a programme for which school-leavers are eligible. Some Community Service Projects are run during the summer, lasting two to four weeks. Minimum age is 18.

Projects work with local organisations to meet community needs and may involve volunteers in activities with mentally and physically handicapped people, with disadvantaged children or environmental work. Volunteers work as part of an international group of 8 to 15 people. No special skills are necessary as training is given. Food and lodging are provided. A small registration fee is charged. Volunteers are responsible for their own fares and pocket money. QVA also has a couple of long-term placements working within the local community with young people starting in January for up to a year.

RADAR

12 City Forum, 250 City Road, London EC1V OAF
Tel: 0207 250 3222   Fax: 020 7250 0212
Email: radar@radar.org.uk   Web: www.radar.org.uk

RADAR was formed in 1977. Members include individuals, organisations of and for people with disabilities, corporate and public-sector organisations. Although work is underrtaken with organisations of all types, RADAR is itself an organisation of disabled people. Those interested in helping disabled people on holidays can contact RADAR, the disability network.

Save the Children

1 St. John's Lane, London EC1M 4AR
Tel: 020 7012 6400   Fax: 020 7012 6963.
Email: supporter.care@savethechildren.org.uk
Web: savethechildren.org.uk

Save the Children fights for children in the UK and around the world who suffer from poverty, disease, injustice and violence. Numerous local and national volunteering opportunities exist, from fundraising to media work.

SHAD (Support and Housing Assistance for People with Disabilities)

5 Bedford Hill, London SW12 9ET
Tel:020 8675 6095
Email:shadwand@aol.com   Web: www.shad.org.uk

SHAD is a London based charity organisation which promotes independent living for people with severe physical disabilities. SHAD requires Voluntary Personal Care Assistants (Pas) to provide physical support to individuals. We provide free accommodation, a weekly allowance, training and support, with excellent work experience. For more details please contact: the Volunteer Development Officer at the address above.

Shelter

88 Old Street London EC1V 9HU
Tel: 020 7505 4699
Email: info@shelter.org.uk   Web: www.shelter.org.uk

Shelter is the national campaigning charity for homeless and badly housed people. From essential research to advising, from court monitoring to garden

makeovers, you could become a Shelter volunteer and make a real difference.
Volunteers may receive help with travel and food expenses.

The Simon Community

PO Box 1187, London NW5 4HW
Tel: 020 7485 6639
Email: info@simoncommunity.org.uk   Web: www.simoncommunity.org.uk

The Simon Community is a community of homeless people and volunteers
living and working with London's street homeless. The community was founded
in 1963 and is a registered charity. Full time volunteers workers live in our
group houses, along with our residents. It's not just about work, it's about living
alongside people. We aim to do outreach work on the streets everyday. Workers
have a separate house to go to on their day off. They also get two weeks holiday
every three months. Workers receive pocket money and holiday allowance.
After 3 months, money is saved up for a leaving allowance. Volunteers need
to be matiure, capable of taking the initiative and able to deal with crises.
The work is challenging and very rewarding. For many of our volunteers it is
a life changing experience. A year spent working in 'Simon' is also regarded
as excellent experience by employers. Length of stay: 3 months to 3 years.
Minimum Age 19 years.

Time for God

2 Chester House, Pages Lane, London N10 1PR
Tel: 020 8883 1504   Fax: 020 8365 2471
Email: office@timeforgod.org   Web: www.timeforgod.org

TFG provides gap years for young adults between the ages of 18-25.
Volunteering opportunities are available for a period of 10-12 months
throughout the UK, USA, Europe, Africa and New Zealand. Opportunities
include gaining experience working in the following: Hostels for homeless
people; Drug rehabilitation centres; Schools / colleges for people with specific
physical / mental needs; Community work with children, young people and
the elderly; Outdoor pursuit centres, and Churches. Board and lodging are
provided plus a weekly personal spending allowance. Training and support
conferences are held for volunteers twice a year, as well as 24hour support from
trained Field Officers. Time for God is is an interdenominational Christian
organisation open to anyone who wants to explore further their personal
Christian faith through action in the community.

Toc H

1 Forest Close, Wendover, Aylesbury, Bucks HP22 6BT
Tel: 01296 623911   Fax: 01296 696137
Email: Info@toch.org.uk   Web: www.toch.org.uk

Toc H runs short-term residential projects through the year in Britain and Belgium, usually from a weekend up to two weeks in duration. Project work undertaken can include: work with people with different disabilities; work with children in need; playschemes and camps; conservation and manual work; and study and/or discussion sessions. These projects provide those who take part with opportunities to learn more about themselves and the world we live in. Whilst foreign applications are welcome, a preference is held for those residing within the European Union. The Toc H projects programme is published yearly. Whilst there is a minimum age limit of 16 years, there is no upper age limit. There is no closing date for applications, but you are advised to apply early. Annual recruitment is 500+.

Treloar Trust

Upper Froyle, Alton, Hants GU34 4JX
Tel: 01420 526526   **Fax: 01420 23957**
Email: info@treloar.org.uk   **Web: www.treloar.org.uk**

The Treloar Trust is a registered charity and our purpose is to provide education, care and training for young people with disabilities. We aim to provide each individual with the support, confidence and skills to achieve the best that they can in all aspects of their lives. This specialist care is provided through Treloar School and Treloar College - centres of excellence which have established an effective, flexible, holistic approach to the education and support of severely disabled young people.

Universal Aunts

PO Box 304, London SW4 ONN
Tel: 020 7738 8937   **Web: www.universalaunts.co.uk**

Established in 1921, Universal Aunts provides men and women for short and long term daily work in the London area. Services cover Nannies, Mother's Helps, Proxy Parents, Child Escorts and Babysitters, Housekeeper/ companions, Cooks, all domestic situtations. Not an au pair agency. Driving licence useful.

Vitalise

12 City Forum, 250 City Road, London, EC1V 8AF
Tel: 0845 345 1972 Fax: 0845 345 1978
Email: info@vitalise.org.uk Web: www.vitalise.org.uk

16 or over? Can you spare a week or two? If yes, we need your help to make a break for disabled adults, children and their carers , at one of the five Vitalise holiday centres in Nottinghamshire, Essex, Merseyside, Southampton and Cornwall. Board and lodging are free, and volunteers help permanent staff in the demanding but worthwhile work of ensuring that guests enjoy a well-planned holiday. This

Five: UK opportunities

can include support and companionship of disabled guests, some domestic chores and accompanying guests on shopping expeditions, trips to theme parks, gardens, the cinema, swimming, ice skating - and even night-clubbing.

Youth Hostels Association

Trevelyan House
Dimple Road, Matlock, Derbyshire, DE4 3YH
Tel: 01629 592600   Fax: 01629 592702
Email: recruitment@yha.org.uk   Web: www.yha.org.uk

YHA offer a number of opportunities for general assistants to work at hostels throughout the UK. Typical responsibilities may include reception, housekeeping and catering. Staff accommodation, discounted food, and free YHA membership are provided during employment.

Environmental organisations

BTCV (British Trust for Conservation Volunteers)

36 St Mary's Street, Wallingford, Oxfordshire OX10 OEU
Tel: 01491 821600   Fax:01491 839646
Email: information@btcv.org   Web: www.btcv.org

BTCV is the UK's largest practical conservation organisation creating opportunities for people of all ages and from all sections of the community to take practical action to protect and improve their local environment. Projects take place throughout the year in England, Wales, Scotland and Northern Ireland and include weekday and weekend projects, training courses and conservation holidays in the UK and overseas. Costs from £30 to £220. Volunteer Officers are always needed at BTCV's 150 offices. The posts may be full-time or part-time for a period of three to 12 months. Work involves supporting the field officer by organising projects, fundraising and carrying out publicity work for the organisation.

Council for British Archaeology

Bowes Morrell House, 111 Walmgate, York YO1 9WA
Tel: 01904 671417   Fax: 01904 671384
Email: info@britarch.ac.uk   Web:www.britarch.ac.uk

The organisation is a non-profit charity set up in 1944 to encourage public interest and understanding of Britain's past. It publishes a regular magazine six times a year, British Archaeology, with an information section, CBA Briefing, giving details of digs around the country requiring volunteers. The April issue usually has the most digs but vacancies are advertised from February. The CBA also produces a series of factsheets on subjects such as Getting Started in Archaeology, and Archaeology in Higher Education. The CBA's information service can provide addresses of many groups and societies to contact for local opportunities. Individual membership of the CBA, with a special full-time student rate, is available. The CBA also coordinates the Young Archaeologists' Club for those aged 9 to 16, which is open to membership for schools.

Cathedral Camps

16 Glebe Avenue, Flitwick, Beds. MK45 IHS
Tel: 01525 716237
Email: admin@cathedralcamps.org.uk   Web: www.cathedralcamps.org.uk

These are one-week camps for those aged between 16 and 30 wishing to help with conservation and maintenance of cathedrals and major parish churches nationally. The venues include most major cathedrals including Canterbury, Durham, Hereford, Worcester, Lincoln, Rochester, Winchester, Truro and Edinburgh. Work is mainly maintenance, clearing roof voids, cleaning windows and painting ironwork etc, but also occasionally includes working with professional conservators on stonework and other architectural features. Projects qualify for the Duke of Edinburgh's Award Scheme. Volunteers pay a contribution towards the cost and accommodation.

Ironbridge Gorge Museums

Ironbridge, Telford, Shropshire TF8 7AW
Tel: 01952 583003 or 433522   Fax:01952 432204
Email: education@ironbridge.org.uk   Web: www.ironbridge.org.uk

There are ten museums in the Ironbridge Gorge interpreting the industries of the Industrial Revolution. Volunteers can get involved in research, education and other general site tasks, but are especially welcomed between March to October to act as demonstrators in Victorian costume at our Blists Hill Victorian Town. Good communication skills are essential and a foreign language would be a real advantage. Potential volunteers must find their own accommodation and transport. Minimum commitment two weeks, maximum three months (could be longer).

National Trust for Scotland

Wemyss House, 28 Charlotte Square, Edinburgh EH2 4ET
Tel: 0131 243 9470   Fax: 0131 243 9593
Email: conservation@nts.org   Web: www.nts.org.uk

The National Trust for Scotland co-ordinates a year long conservation volunteer programme which is carried out through the running of working holidays and weekend projects on NTS properties all over Scotland. Four local Conservation Volunteer groups (Glasgow, Lothian, Tayside, Grampian) carry out practical conservation work on weekend projects throughout the year. A wide range of tasks is tackled including footpath management, scrub clearance, fencing, dyking and tree planting. All projects contribute to the care and protection of Scotland's countryside, wildlife and archaeology. All weekend projects are free. Food, accommodation and transport are provided. Between April and October of each year volunteers from as far away as Australia and from all ages and backgrounds take part in NTS residential working conservation holidays called Thistle Camps. Projects last between one and two weeks and are based at breathtaking and often remote locations throughout Scotland. The work is wide ranging and interesting as the camps offer opportunities to learn specific skills such as archaeology, species management and footpath repair. Much sought-after are our camps on Fair Isle, Burg, Iona and Mar Lodge Estate. For details contact the above or request pack from website.

National Trust Working Holidays

33 Sheep Street, Cirencester, Glos GL7 1RQ
Tel: 0870 609 5383 Fax:01285 657935
Email:volunteer@ntrust.org.uk
Web: www.nationaltrust.org.uk/volunteering

People aged 16 and over (no upper limit) can spend periods of a week on a National Trust site helping with conservation tasks which could not otherwise be done. The programme runs all year and includes more than 470 projects at locations all over England and Wales, each of which can take about a dozen volunteers. They last 2 to 7 days and work may include woodland management, restoring pasture, fencing, path construction, bridge building, stone-walling, clearing lakes and streams, gardening, botanical surveys, and so on. Volunteers pay £55 towards the cost of food and accommodation for the project. A free brochure is available from the above address or can be found online.

RSPB (Royal Society for the Protection of Birds)

The Lodge, Sandy, Bedfordshire SG19 2DL
Tel: 01767 680551   **Fax: 01767 692365**
Web: www.rspb.org.uk/vacancies

The RSPB is the largest wildlife conservation charity in Europe. The RSPB manages 176 reserves in England, Scotland, Wales and Northern Ireland covering over 121,000 hectares, protecting important habitats and rare or threatened birds. The Society undertakes detailed research, seeks to influence decision-makers, educates and informs over 1 million members and helps to develop international conservation projects. From age 16 you can apply to be a Voluntary Warden on a reserve.

Work may include escorting visitors, assisting with research and physical management such as cutting vegetation, maintaining paths and clearing ditches under the supervision of the warden. Accommodation is provided, but you must supply your own food, pocket money and make your own travel arrangements to the reserve. The minimum period is one week and the maximum is four weeks for new volunteers. Longer periods can be negotiated thereafter. The scheme operates all year round. Ornithological skills are not required. For an information pack and application form please write to: The Voluntary Warden Scheme, Youth and Volunteers Department (OIG) at the above address, enclosing two 1st class stamps and self-addressed label. A limited number of paid, contract summer wardens are required, age 20 or over. Applications are invited from competent ornithologists with practical conservation skills. Further details from the Personnel Department at the above address or visit the Web.

The Wildlife Trust

The Welsh Wildlife Centre, Cilgerrán, Cardigan SA43 2TB
Tel: 01239 621600   **Fax: 01239 613211**
Email:wildlife@wtww.co.uk   **Web:www.wtww.co.uk**

A non-profit making organisation which manages 67 nature reserves including the seabird islands of Skokholm and Skomer. It takes on a few voluntary assistant wardens annually between March and October on Skomer for a maximum of two-three weeks. Work includes maintenance of buildings, hides and footpaths, receiving day visitors to the island and collecting landing fees. No special skills needed, but need to be fit and able to work long hours if necessary. Basic accommodation available; volunteers provide their own food. Free return passage to Skomer from mainland provided. Applications usually from 1 September for the following year. Requests to be sent to the Islands Booking Officer at the above address - apply early. There are also opportunities for residential volunteers at the Wildlife Centre itself. Volunteers stay free of charge in the bunkhouse but pay for food and transport. Apply a few months before you wish to go.

Activity centres

3D Education and Adventure

Osmington Bay Centre, Shortlake Lane, Weymouth, Dorset DT3 6EG
Tel: 01305 836226   **Fax: 01305 834070**
Email: admin@3d-jobs.co.uk   **Web: www.3d.co.uk**

We are looking for energetic, fun and bubbly people who are interested in rewarding work over the months of July and August. The position of monitor is best suited to those either starting university in September, or those of you who are already at university but will be available during your summer holidays. However, as long as you're over 18 and you have a desire to work with children then we'd like to hear from you.

Camp Beaumont

The Old Rectory, Beeston Regis, Norfolk NR27 9NG
Tel. No: 01263 823000
Email: info@campbeaumont.com   Web: www.campbeaumont.com

Camp Beaumont operates operate day camps at nine centres in the London area, These offer children and young people between 3 and 15 the opportunity to experience a wide range of outdoor activities. To ensure that a safe, fun packed and exciting environment is created, we employ Group Leaders, Activity Instructors, Senior Nursery Leaders, Nursery Leaders and Senior Group Leaders for a period of between 5-6 weeks during July and August. All applicants should be caring, active and outgoing individuals, with a sound education, who enjoy the outdoors and want to work with children. Camp Beaumont also operate residential activity camps at four UK locations. There are opportunities for group leaders and instructors for the summer period. Some posts require basic childcare qualifications. Comprehensive training is provided. Full details and application information is available on the website.

Center Parcs (UK)

Kirklington Rd, Eakring, Newark, Nottinghamshire NG22 0DZ
Tel : 01623 872 300   Fax: 01623 872 442
Web: www.centerparcs.co.uk

Occasional opportunities for gap students at the four UK holiday villages. Jobs may be routine to start with, but in-company training is possible. Please note that accommodation is not usually provided. Application forms for each of the following Centre Parcs locations can be downloaded from the website.

- Elveden Forest, Brandon, Suffolk IP27 0YZ Tel: 01842 894802
- Oasis Whinfell Forest, Temple Sowerby, Cumbria CA10 2DW Tel: 01768 893004
- Longleat Forest, Warminster, Wiltshire BA12 7PU Tel: 01985 848343
- Sherwood Forest, Rufford, Newark, Nottinghamshire NG22 9DN Tel: 01623 827417

PGL Travel Ltd

Alton Court, Penyard Lane, Ross-on-Wye, Herefordshire HR9 5NR
Tel: 0870 401 4411
Email: pglpeople@pgl.co.uk   Web: www.pgl.co.uk/gapyear

PGL runs adventure holidays and courses in the UK (and also in France and Spain) for young people aged 7-17. The main activities are canoeing, sailing, windsurfing, abseiling and, plus a wide range of other activities including climbing, pony trekking, challenge courses and archery. Some Instructional posts require relevant experience or instructor qualifications. To be a Group

Leader (who look after the children outside of activity sessions), you need experience of working with/looking after children. There are also a range of jobs requiring no previous experience, including Site or Catering Assistants, Domestics and Tuck Shop staff. Food and accommodation are provided in addition to a living allowance.

The PGL season lasts from February to November. You can apply to work for this full period, for as little as eight weeks or for any period in between. Some vacancies, including at Southern French and Spanish centres, are for shorter-term contracts, from April - September. The website includes comprehensive information about UK and international employment opportunities, including online application facilities.

Thorpe Park Leisure Park and Chessington World of Adventure

HR Department, PO Box 125, Chessington KT9 2WL
Tel: 0870 444 4466
Email: via website   Web: www.thorpepark.co.uk

Temporary positions are available from March to November in the following departments: marketing, rides and attractions, visitor services, audit, cleaning, personnel, retail, bank, farm, entertainments. Some of these could be particularly useful for gap year students or undergraduates taking vocational courses. Full details from the address above or on the website.

Other opportunities

Accenture Horizons Gap Year Scheme

60 Queen Victoria Street, London EC4N 4TW
Tel: 0207 844 4000   Fax: 0 207 844 4444
Email: via website   Web: www.accenture.com

Accenture is a global management consulting and technology services company employing 100,000 people in 48 countries. The scheme provides students looking to take a gap year with a unique combination of training and work experience. The scheme lasts eight months, from September to April each year, and offers a competitive salary.

At Your Service

12 Talina Centre, Bagleys Lane, London SW6 2BW
Tel: 020 7610 8610   Fax: 020 76108611
Email: london@ays.co.uk   Web: www.ays.co.uk

Specialist in the provision of staff to outside caterers, event organisers, production companies, PR companies and private clients. Short term opportunities may be available.

Five: UK opportunities

Black & Veatch Consulting Ltd

Grosvenor House, 69 London Road, Redhill, Surrey RH1 1LQ
Tel: 01737 774 155   Fax: 01737 772 767
Email: via website   Web: www.bvcs.bv.com

Consulting civil engineers specialising in water supply, waste water, energy services and environmental engineering. Limited gap year opportunities may be available each year for an interesting range of applied science and mathematical modelling. Suitable for candidates with maths and physics A levels intending to read for engineering, maths or physics degrees.

British Broadcasting Corporation

BBC Recruitment Services, PO Box 7000, London W1A 6GJ
Tel: 020 8740 333 1330
Email: recruitment@bbc.co.uk   Web: www.bbc.co.uk

Can offer one year's pre-university training in Research and Development. Applicants must be intending to read for an electronic engineering degree, physics, software engineering or similar. Students will be based in Surrey and will receive a salary. Contact BBC Recruitment Services.

Data Connection Ltd

100 Church Street Enfield Middlesex EN2 6BQ
Tel: 020 8366 1177
Email: recruit@dataconnection.com   Web: www.dataconnection.com

Data Connection is a world class computer technology company with a unique reputation for developing complex high quality software on time, to tight deadlines. Our customers include IBM, Microsoft and BT, as well as smaller technology start-ups. Our success is based on our ability to employ outstandingly talented individuals, including students who want to work either during a year out or over the summer before going to university. As a pre-university student you will be given challenging assignments with plenty of support and expert guidance to encourage you to develop your technical and organisational skills. If you do really well you may be offered university sponsorship. We look for talented students (those who have, or are expecting, all A grades at A level), who have a keen interest in the application of computer technology. In return we offer a salary and subsidised accommodation in one of our Company Houses. All we ask is that you work for a minimum of eight weeks - in fact, many choose to stay for up to a year.

Deloitte Scholars Scheme

Stonecutter Court, 1 Stonecutter St, London EC4A 4TR
Tel: 020 7303 7019
Email: hmanthorpe@deloitte.co.uk   Web: www.deloitte.co.uk/scholars

Deloitte & Touche LLP, a worldwide professional services organisation, offers lucrative and challenging gap year work along with continued sponsorship through univeristy. The scheme includes a 30-week paid placement in a UK office plus a £1,500 pre-university travel bursary, additional paid placements and annual bursary payments of £1,000 each academic year.

IBM United Kingdom Limited

Student Recruitment, IBM UK Ltd, PO Box 41, F2Q North Harbour, Portsmouth PO6 3AU
Tel: 02392 561000
Email: student_pgms@uk.ibm.com Web: ibm.com/uk/employment

If you are looking for a gap year before university a year with IBM will provide you with far more than work experience. As the world´s largest IT company, we have more options for people like you, simply because we have more training initiatives for talented young individuals and more complex issues to test fresh ideas and energy. We have a large, vibrant student community and can offer technical and non technical roles around the UK for a 9 - 12 month duration. For more information on the scheme go to www.ibm.com/employment/uk

Institute of Physics

Institute of Physics, 76 Portland Place, London W1B 1NT
Tel: 020 7470 4800   **Fax: 020 7470 4848**
Email: education@iop.org   **Web: www.iop.org**

This organisation publishes a sponsorship and work placement booklet listing companies which are able to offer sponsorship to physics undergraduates - but It also lists companies offering work placements, either to school students or undergraduates. Contact the Education Department.

PricewaterhouseCoopers

No 1 London Bridge, London SE1 9QL
Tel: 020 7804 2466   **Fax: 020 7804 3030**
Email: via website   **Web: www.pricewaterhousecoopers.co.uk**

Running for seven months from September to March, the PwC Gap Year Programme is open to high-calibre students who are looking to take time out between school and university. You could be looking to earn some money to ease the financial burden of your studies. Or raise the funds you need to go travelling before you start your degree. Either way, we think you'll find spending seven months with us is extremely productive. The opportunities available depend on the area of our business you're interested in. Firstly, you could join us in Assurance & Business Advisory Services (ABAS) at our Bristol, London, Uxbridge, Reading, Maidstone or Southampton offices.

Alternatively, you could join Tax & Legal Services (TLS), however this is only available at one of our London offices. We also recruit one actuarial student in London each year.

European Engineering Foundation (Smallpeice Trust)

74 Upper Holly Walk, Leamington Spa, Warwickshire CV32 4JL
Tel: 01926 333200   Fax: 01926 333202
Email: gen@smallpeicetrust.org.uk   Web: www.smallpeicetrust.org.uk

For students of engineering this really is the pinnacle of gap years. It provides a unique combination of study, language tuition, travel and work experience in Europe. The course is intensive, demanding and wholly enjoyable - not only an important stepping stone in the career development of young engineers but a truly memorable experience to carry through life. The Smallpeice Trust is responding to the UK and Europe's need for engineering students of the highest calibre, ultimately to fill the top jobs in the engineering industry.

The course aims to give students a firm grounding in different engineering disciplines combined with the relevant management skills. Students additionally benefit from an enhanced programme to improve their language, experience the culture of another country, and enjoy personal and career development. The course is not designed to replace all or part of university education, but to complement it.Applications are invited from A level, CSYS higher, BTEC or equivalent students who will complete their examinations in summer 2005 and who wish to take a gap year by deferring their entry to university on an engineering-related degree course. Applicants must be 18 years old at the start of the programme.

Tillinghast-Towers Perrin

Graduate Recruitment, Towers Perrin, 71 High Holborn, London WC1V 6TP
Telephone: 020 7170 2000
Email: act_grads@towers.com   Web: www.tillinghast.com

Towers Perrin (including Tillinghast-Towers Perrin) is one of the world's largest independent consulting firms specialising in Actuarial and Human Resource consulting. We employ over 800 actuaries globally and in the actuarial field we provide high quality consultancy services on all aspects of employee benefits, financial services and general insurance. Tillinghast-Towers Perrin has gap year opportunities for students wishing to take a year out prior to commencing university. Vacancies are within the general insurance actuarial practice, based in London, and provide students with the opportunity to gain valuable experience in a dynamic environment. Actuaries use their analytical powers, mathematical tools, economic knowledge, statistical concepts and judgement to forecast future events and conditions. They apply probability and statistics to financial matters. Positions are for approximately nine months, commencing in September and ending in May the following year. You should be expecting at least a grade B at A level mathematics and two other high grade A levels. You will also be intending to undertake a numerate degree at university. You will receive comprehensive training as required, including IT training. Application is by CV and covering letter by post or email, or you can apply on-line.

The Year in Industry

Technology House, Salford University Business Park, Lissadel Street, Salford M6 6AP

Tel: 0161 278 2497   **Fax: 0161 278 2497**
Email:enquiries@yini.org.uk   **Web: www.yini.org.uk**

There has never been a stronger case for taking a gap year in industry, not just for the experience and the head start for graduate employment, but also to earn money to help you through university, and the chance of sponsorship or paid vacation work. The Year in Industry is the largest single provider of gap year industrial placements. Over 300 companies regularly take part, from 'blue chip' multinationals to small/medium-sized enterprises. Placements span a wide range of industries, from biotechnology to transportation, from research and consultancy to energy and electronics. There are regional centres right across England, Scotland and Wales. Check the website or contact the National Director at the above address for further details.

NOTE FOR TRAVELLERS

You will obviously consult your own doctor about any necessary health precautions and inoculations you might need. MASTA (Medical Advisory Service for Travellers Abroad) set up by the London School of Tropical Medicine offer a range of health services for travellers.
Web: www.masta.org   Tel: 0113 238 7500   Email enquiries@masta.org

The Foreign and Commonwealth Office provides information for British nationals travelling abroad and living overseas on their website at www.fco.gov.uk - select Travel option from the Services menu.

For more information about planning, safety and health issues please refer to entries in Section Three

Looking for opportunities overseas

M any gap students like the idea of working for a time abroad. Some countries like the USA have very strict visa regulations, making it difficult to work legally except through government approved schemes. Paid work in developing countries and Eastern Europe is also very hard to come by. There are several very useful books on the market which offer general advice on job-hunting in individual countries, with names and addresses of agencies and employers, plus titles of relevant newspapers, magazines, directories etc.

A useful website is **www.workingabroad.com** This is an international networking service for volunteers, workers and travellers, covering 150 countries. WorkingAbroad researches and compiles documentation for volunteers on opportunities throughout the world, aiming to provide a comprehensive information service on a wide variety of possibilities for each volunteer.

Early application for many of these jobs is essential. If you leave it until after you leave school you may well find that all the best jobs have gone, so start thinking about it at Christmas the year before you leave. Check the closing date for applications in the following entries where these are given. Even if you do miss out, it may still be possible to find work by going to the country and looking on-the-spot, but you may well end up being over-worked and under-paid.

Many of the voluntary work opportunities are also filled before the summer, so again you should make contact with organisations that interest you in good time. Note when the annual brochures are published and make sure you send for yours at once. It is not easy to find the time to do this in the run up to exams, but a well-planned gap is likely to give the most satisfaction - and enhance your CV.

The majority of opportunities for voluntary work abroad are for graduates and newly-qualified professional people aged 21 and over. However, some opportunities are to be found, mainly with religious organisations.

Notes on working with children

For general advice on becoming an au pair, regulations in different countries, problems that may occur and how to set about job hunting, consult The Au Pair and Nanny's Guide to Working Abroad *(see Further Information)*.

Agencies tend to come and go, so there is no guarantee that any of those listed here or in the above book will still be in business a year or two from now. A few, however, are very long-established.

NB: the US government has regulations concerning the care of very young children. No-one is allowed to work with children aged under two years unless they have documented evidence of at least 200 hours experience in the last three years. Additionally, all au pairs have to undergo a 32 hour orientation course approved by the government held in the US on arrival.

Notes on working in Australia

Working holiday visas are available for up to 12 months. Citizens from eligible countries who are aged between 18 and 30 years old and without any dependent children are eligible to apply for a Working Holiday Visa. Further information is available on the internet (www.australia.org.uk/ahc/html/index.html). The Australian High Commission office in London is at Australia House, Strand, London WC2B 4LA. Anyone wanting to spend a pre-university period in Australia is advised to apply to the following organisations:

- *GAP Ltd* (see entry later in this section)

- **BUNAC** (see entry later in this section) runs a WORK AUSTRALIA programme for those over 18 and under 26.

- **CIEE** (Council on International Educational Exchange) runs a similar AUSTRALIA WORK AND TRAVEL PROGRAMME. CIEE works with a world-wide network of partners to bring our work and study programs to thousands of students, graduates and young people every year. The CIEEpartner/contact organisation in the UK is: **IST Plus Ltd** (see later entry in this section). CIEE's Work & Travel Australia program helps Working Holiday Visa holders make the most of their time in Australia. From providing a meet and greet service, to use of the Exchange HQ facilities at our office in central Sydney, the program gives participants access to all the information and advice that they need to find accommodation and work in Australia. Through Exchange HQ participants can also book excursions and activities, as well as enrol on language or other study courses. We have a comprehensive website dedicated to the Work & Travel Australia program (www.workinaustralia.net/index.html). Work & Travel Australia also comes under the umbrella of the American Institute for Foreign Study (AIFS).

- Travellers to Australia can arrange placements on-the-spot with **Conservation Volunteers Australia (CVA)**, National Head Office, PO Box 423, Ballarat, Victoria 3353 Tel: +61 3 5330 2600 or Free call within Australia: 1800032501 Email:info@conservatonvolunteers.com.au Web:www.conservationvolunteers.com.au CVA aims to attract and manage a force of volunteers in practical conservation projects for the betterment of the Australian environment. Our volunteers come from a wide range of backgrounds, and you don't need any prior skills or experience. We have volunteer opportunities to suit your availability and interest.

Classification

Many of the organisations listed in this section offer both short-term and long-term opportunities. A number of providers also combine community and conservation projects. The entries in this section have therefore been listed in alphabetical order, but with locations and other key words highlighted for easier reading.

Africa and Asia Venture

10 Market Place, Devizes, Wiltshire SN10 1HT
Tel: 01380 729 009   Fax: 01380 720 060
Email: av@aventure.co.uk   Web: www.aventure.co.uk

Africa and Asia Venture sends British school leavers to K*enya, Uganda, Tanzania, Malawi, Botswana, Mexico, India* and *Nepal* for about four months between school and further education. Its aim is to enable students to work and experience life in Africa and Asia. Volunteers are placed in pairs in either carefully selected schools for a one term attachment as Assistant Teachers or in other community or conservation related projects in Kenya. There is an in-country four day orientation course prior to the attachment and a three week travel period, including an organised group "safari" at the end, giving volunteers an opportunity to travel more widely in the country. The cost is approximately £2590 (2004/05) which includes insurance, accommodation, living allowances and the all-inclusive "safari", but not airfares to your destination. Volunteers must be aged over seventeen and nine months at the time of departure. Application should be made as early as possible. For more details contact the Director at the above address.

African Conservation Experience

PO Box 206, Faversham, Kent ME13 8WZ
Tel: 0870 241 5816
Web: www.conservationafrica.net/

We can offer you the chance to work on Game and Nature Reserves alongside Conservationists, Zoologists, Wildlife Vets and Reserve Managers. We welcome volunteers from all backgrounds, with no previous experience necessary, from the age of 17 upwards. Placements are from 1-3 months, and you can combine 2 or more projects in one trip. Join us for the experience of a lifetime in Africa and make a genuine contribution to the preservation of one of the World's most diverse and vulnerable ecosystems.

• Work in *Big 5 country in the heart of the African bush*
• Get involved in Game Capture for tagging and relocation
• Veterinary work
• Behavioural studies on Lions and Elephants, Whale and Dolphin research
• Rehabilitation of orphaned animals
• Learn how horses are used for conservation
• Discover the thrill of Sleep-Outs under the African stars
• Complete a Game Ranger Guide course
• Rewarding Cultural Placement. Help with whatever you are good at! Teaching, Sports, Music, Computers...

You can apply online. Travel costs and food arrangements vary from reserve to reserve and according to the time of year. Some projects cost from as little as

£1850 for 4 weeks. Most students can expect to pay about £2,700 for 4 weeks up to some £3,900 for a 12 week placement. This includes international flights, domestic transfers in Africa, full board throughout your stay.

Agriventure

Servicing Offices, IAEA/AgriVenture, Speedwell Farm Bungalow, Nettle Bank, Wisbech, Cambridgeshire PE14 0SA
Tel: 01945 450999
Email:uk@agriventure.com   Web: www.agriventure.com

Agriventure is run by the International Agricultural Exchange Association (IAEA). It offers travel and work opportunities in 12 different countries in *Europe, Asia, North America, Australia* and *New Zealand* for young people aged between 18-30 who are interested in agriculture or horticulture. From the UK/Europe you can go to Australia, New Zealand, Canada, USA or Japan. Programmes can last from 4 months to over a year. As a trainee you would stay with a host family on a farm or horticultural enterprise, working on one of several programmes in agriculture, horticulture, home management (working around the home) or a mixture of agriculture or horticulture and home. Trainees need to have some practical farming or horticulture experience and have a current full driving licence. The scheme is particularly suitable for students intending to train for a land-based career. The cost of joining a programme ranges from around £2000 to Canada and £2500 to New Zealand. This includes flights, insurance, full board and accommodation, a 24-hour emergency support service, an orientation seminar in your host country and transport to the farm. You will be paid an allowance and the hours of work are regulated. You will be able to travel during the holiday period of your trip and can arrange to holiday with other trainees.

L'Arche

10 Briggate, Silsden, Keighley, West Yorkshire BD20 9JT
Tel: 01535 656186   Fax: 01535 656426
Email: info@larche.org.uk   Web: www.larche.org/

L'Arche Communities are places where people with learning disabilities and their assistants live and work together very much as family and friends. Founded by Jean Vanier, L'Arche is an international network of communities comprising over 124 communities in 30 countries. Opportunities exist mainly in *Europe* and *North America* for applicants without previous experience of L'Arche. In-service training, free board and lodging and pocket money provided. No qualifications are needed, though craft and domestic skills are useful. Although Christian in practice, L'Arche welcomes people from other faiths or none. Most Communities look for a minimum commitment of 12 months. Contact the Company Secretary of L'Arche UK, at the above address for further information and a full list of world-wide communities. A registered charity

Aupair in America

37 Queens Gate, London SW7 5HR
Tel: 020 7581 7322   **Fax: 020 7581 7345**
Web: www.aupairinamerica.co.uk

This was set up by the American Institute for Foreign Study (AIFS) and is the largest agency. Au pairs can stay in the *USA* for a year and earn $139 a week. They must all take some form of study while in the country and they have opportunities to travel inside the country. See also entry for Camp America (location in index). There are two other programmes running alongside Au Pair in America:

AU PAIR EXTRAORDINAIRE – if you have a recognised childcare qualification or 2 years' recent full-time childcare experience, then you may qualify for our Au Pair Extraordinaire programme, earning US$200 a week.

EDUCARE IN AMERICA – offers the added benefit of a formal educational programme and fewer childcare hours looking after school age children. With EduCare in America you get a taste of the college experience without having to pay high fees, while earning a weekly payment and enjoying the support of a caring family. EduCare in America is also located at 37 Queen's Gate, Tel: 020 7581 7363, Email: info@educareamerica.co.uk .

Blue Ventures

52 Avenue Road, London N6 5DR
Tel: 020 8341 9819   **Fax: 020 8341 4821**
Email: volunteer@blueventures.org   **Web: www.blueventures.org**

Blue Ventures is a UK-based not-for-profit organisation, dedicated to facilitating projects that enhance global coral reef conservation and research. Since its creation Blue Ventures has co-ordinated marine projects in *Madagascar, Tanzania, New Zealand, South Africa* and the *Comoros Islands*. Our research fulfils a priority of the international coral reef initiative, and is also considered a priority within the framework for the national strategy for the conservation of biodiversity in Madagascar, the site of our principal research projects.

Volunteers from all over the world and from all walks of life work with us both above and below the water, and are responsible for a range of tasks, from carrying out field research to managing the day-to-day running of field camps. We will charge each volunteer £1780 for a 6-week expedition. For the first week, consisting of diving training, the cost will be £400 (Optional). For the second week, consisting of scientific training, the cost will be £430 (Compulsory). For the remaining four weeks the cost will be £950. Kit, flights and visas are not included. We welcome applications from volunteers of all ages, backgrounds and nationalities.

The Bridge

Friends of Israel Educational Foundation, PO Box 7545, London, NW2 2QZ
Tel: 020 7435 6803   Fax: 020 7794 0291
Email: info@foi-asg.org   Web: www.foi-asg.org/gap1.htm

Up to 12 school leavers each year are offered passages to *Israel* and free board and lodging for five months. Each Bridge schedule includes a working place on a kibbutz (collective farm), two months community service in a development town/Israeli new town, work in a northern Israeli moshav (smallholders' co-operative), contact with the many communities constituting modern Israel, seminars and organised tours, free time to explore *Jordan* and *Egypt,* experience of an archaeological dig - an optional extra - at the participant's expense. Qualification is by a minimum 400 word essay and an interview. No knowledge of Hebrew required and places are open to all boys and girls, irrespective of religion.

BTCV

163 Balby Road, Doncaster, South Yorkshire. DN4 0RH
Tel: 01302 572 244   Fax: 01302 310 167
Email:information@btcv.org.uk   Web: www.btcv.org

To add to its UK-based Conservation Holidays, BTCV has developed a programme of *International Conservation Holidays.* UK volunteers are invited to join members of local communities in a network of cultural and ecological conservation projects, lasting between two and three weeks. Holidays include trail blazing in the *USA*, trail work & wilderness management in *Iceland*, traditional building restoration in *Greece*, rare bird rescue in *Bulgaria* and waterfall path and plantlife survey in *Lesotho*. There are dozens of holidays in over 25 countries worldwide. Minimum age 18. BTCV International Conservation Holidays cost from £220-£1450 depending on destination and holiday duration. (NB. unless otherwise stated, the holiday price given does not include travel).

BUNAC

16 Bowling Green Lane, London EC1R 0QH
Tel: 020 7251 3472 Fax: 020 7251 0215
Email: enquiries@bunac.org.uk   Web: www.bunac.org.uk

BUNAC (The British Universities North America Club) is a non-profit organisation established in 1962 to enable young people to participate actively in the North American way of life through work and travel. It runs a number of different schemes.

(1) KAMP offers full-time students the opportunity to work on *American children's summer camps* in ancillary positions. Currently, you are not eligible to apply if you are a final year university student or a gap year (i.e.

between school and university) student. Check the website for changes to KAMP eligibility.

(2) SUMMER CAMP USA employs people aged 18/19 to 35 as camp counsellors (for details see Section 5). They are paid around $820 for 9 weeks and the cost of flights is deducted at the end.

(3) WORK CANADA To be eligible for the 2005 **Work Canada programme** as a student, you must be aged 18-30 and a current full-time student on a degree level course or equivalent (such as HND or NVQ level 4 or 5) or, a gap year student with a guaranteed place at university starting in 2005. Typical jobs include: Shop assistant, Ski lift operator, Office supervisor, Ski resort rep, Hotel receptionist, Chambermaid, Waiting on tables. You are not restricted to this type of work however. The Work Authorisation is flexible and allows you to look for other types of work.

(4) WORK AMERICA is a similar scheme for which currently, you are not eligible to apply if you are a final year university student or a gap year (i.e. between school and university) student. Check the website for changes to Work America eligibility.

(5) BUNAC also runs similar schemes for work/travel in **Australia and New Zealand**, suitable for gap year students.

(6) GAP **Canada** is specifically for pre-university gap year students aged 18-20. Departures are October-December.

(7) VOLUNTEER **GHANA** provides a unique opportunity for young people to work in a community based project for 3 - 6 months while living alongside the Ghanaian people. You must be a recent university graduate (within two years of graduation), a gap year student or a current university student.

For other opportunities see the website.

Camp America

37a Queen's Gate, London SW7 5HR, UK
Tel: 0207 581 7373   **Fax: 0 207 581 7377**
Email: enquiries@campamerica.co.uk   Web: www.campamerica.co.uk

Camp America is the largest pre-arranged summer work experience in the world. The organisation is recognised by the US Department of State as a sponsor of people aged 18 and over whom it places as 'counsellors' in children's summer camps **throughout America**. Those selected leave for America by late June to work for 9 weeks with the option of travelling independently for a further 10 weeks until October. Work consists of supervising a group of children, instructing a specific activity, such as swimming, tennis, arts or riding, or looking after the day-to-day care of a group and helping in the general running of the camp. There are also openings for 'special needs counsellors'., Air transport, room, board and pocket money are all provided by Camp America. Another programme which is offered is 'campower'where participants help with the kitchen/maintenance/office side of camp for nine weeks. Camp America can also place applicants with American families as 'au pairs' (The Au Pair in America programme, see index for location) or on an American holiday resort (minimum age 19). A new programme 'Work Adventures' allows you to either find your own placement (Adventure option) or they will do it for you (Explorer option). They will make all the necessary arrangements about flights, visas, insurance etc.to receive more information call the number above or visit the Web.

Camps International Ltd

Unit 1 Kingfisher Park, Headlands Business Park, Salisbury Road, Blashford, Ringwood BH24 3NX
Tel: 0870 2401843   **Fax: 01425 485398**
Email: info@campsinternational.com   Web: www.campsinternational.com

Camps International has developed a safari camp concept specifically for gap year travellers joining a 1 - 3 month, project based package focused entirely on **East Africa**. They provide a safe, team environment in the bush providing clients with comfortable walk-in tents, good food and truly international social life. Clients spend the majority of the week working on a selection of community projects ranging from teaching to construction and conservation initiatives in and around the Parks. Weekend activities such as walking safaris to night game drives are available on request. Adventurous challenges include **Kilimanjaro, Mt Kenya** and Scuba Diving with a strong focus on quality as opposed to budget. CAMP KENYA 1 (CK1) - previously Gap 28 - is a one month package, CAMP KENYA 2 (CK2) is for 2 months and CAMP KENYA 3 (CK3) is a 3 month placement. The new Camp Tanzania will be similar in format to Camp Kenya and fully operational by January 2006.

Canvas Holidays

12 Abbey Park Place, Dunfermline, Fife, Scotland KY12 7PD
Tel: 01383 629018   **Fax: 01383 620481**
Web: www.canvasholidays.co.uk/recruitment/recruit-index.asp

Canvas Holidays are the originators of self-drive camping holidays, established over 30 years ago, providing fully equipped, ready-erected frame tents and mobile homes for around 56,000 customers across Europe, every summer. The majority of sites are in France but there are also sites in **Italy, Spain, Austria, Germany** and **Luxembourg**. Canvas Holidays would like to hear from responsible, independent individuals and couples of all ages, minimum age is 18 years old (19 years in France), who would be interested in working as residential couriers from end-March to mid-October. Strenuous physical work is involved in the putting up of the tents (which couriers do in teams) and in the day-to-day care of the equipment. Couriers must also be able to deal with any problems that the holidaymakers may encounter, and must also maintain good working relations with the campsite manager and staff. Children's couriers are also employed on many sites. Tented accommodation is provided, insurance cover arranged and all our overseas staff will go through a comprehensive training course upon arrival abroad.. You will need at least one years experience of working with the public and knowledge of a foreign language is preferred, although not essential. The ability to speak a major European language is preferred but not essential. Apply online or phone for application pack.

CCUSA

1st Floor N, Devon House, 171 Great Portland Street, London W1W5PQ
Tel: 0207 637 0779   **Fax: 0207 580 6209**
Email facility online   **Web: www.ccusa.com**

Camp Counselors USA places you at a summer camp which matches your personality, skills and interest, where you work for a minimum of nine weeks. When your camp assignment ends, you are free to travel independently in the USA for up to seven weeks before you return home. CCUSA is designated by the *United States* State Department as an official exchange visitor program sponsor. As such, CCUSA is authorized to issue the official forms necessary for J-1 cultural exchange visas. Criteria for eligibility include:
• Do you genuinely enjoy working with or around children?
• Are you outgoing, cheerful, adaptable, flexible, cooperative and diligent?
• Will you be at least 18 years of age by June 1st?
See the website for details and eligibility criteria of other programmes.

Changing Worlds

11 Doctors Lane, Chaldon, Surrey CR3 5AE
Tel: 01883 340960   **Fax: 01883 330783**
Email: welcome@changingworlds.co.uk Web: changingworlds.co.uk

Changing Worlds offers challenging voluntary work placements in *Tanzania, Chile, India, Nepal and Romania*. To succeed you must have drive and a desire to make a real contribution. "The hardest thing I have ever done but the best thing I have done" is how returned volunteer Beth Woodger summarised her time at an orphanage in *Southern India*. Most volunteers teach although there are a growing number of care work placements in orphanages. Volunteers with sport, music and drama are always popular. After a 2-day briefing in the UK volunteers travel out as a group to their destinations where they are taken to the orientation and basic language course run by the representative. After a few days volunteers go in small groups to live and work in local schools and projects.

Changing Worlds prides itself on being a small organisation that knows each volunteer; assistance is always available in-country and in the UK. Prices start from £1,795 and include return flight and transfer to the placement, courses, accommodation, and all UK and overseas support. Additionally volunteers must budget for visas, insurance, pocket money and some food in certain cases. Fundraising advice is given at interview.

Changing Worlds also offer **paid work in Canada, Australia,** and **New Zealand.** Working in Canada is in the Canadian Rockies in a variety of top end hotels. The work is reasonably paid and allows workers the opportunity to snowboard or ski on their days off as well as gaining very well regarded work experience in a highly customer focused environment. In New Zealand there is hotel work too in three attractive locations including a ski resort and a seaside resort. Changing Worlds' paid workers in Australia work in hotels, for a minimum of thirty hours per week and a proper wage. The zoo and farming placements in Australia are voluntary placements. Applicants need to be aged between 18 and 30 years old to gain a working holiday visa for Australia. Information pack can be requested online and applications welcome online.

Childcare International Ltd

Trafalgar House, Grenville Place, London NW7 3SA
Freephone: 0800 652 0020   Tel: 020 8906 3116   Fax: 020 8906 3461
Email: office@childint.co.uk   Web: www.childint.com

(i) Childcare Europe scheme for au pairs, mother's helps, etc. in **Europe.** Full supervision of local partner agency. Full or part time positions available. Minimum six month commitment. Childcare experience preferred.

(ii) Childcare America – Childcare International is one of two partner agencies in the UK representing AU PAIR IN AMERICA, offering a one year stay with a carefully selected host family. Fares to and from the **United States**, fees for classes at local educational institutions and $139 pocket money a week provided plus medical insurance. Four day Orientation in Connecticut USA prior to joining host family. Full support network in America, local friends and many leisure opportunities. A counsellor is on hand throughout the year to sort out any problems. Experience with children and a full driving licence essential.

(iii) Childcare **Australia** - Through associated agencies can arrange mother's help positions lasting 6 - 12 months. Full back-up from local representative.

Concordia International Volunteer Projects

Heversham Hse, 20-22 Boundary Rd, Hove, E Sussex BN3 4ET
Tel: 01273 422218   Fax: 01273 421182
Email: info@concordia-iye.org.uk   Web: www.concordia-iye.org.uk

Concordia is a small not-for-profit youth charity whose aims are to encourage international youth exchange as a means of promoting greater cultural awareness, international understanding and peace. Short-term international volunteer projects are one way by which we hope to achieve these aims.

Our International Volunteer Programme offers the opportunity to join international teams of volunteers working on short-term projects in over 30 countries world-wide. You must be between 18 and 30 years of age unless a specific project states otherwise. For all North/South projects you should be over 20.

The project range is diverse and includes nature conservation, restoration, archaeology, construction, art and culture as well as projects that are more socially based including work with adults or children with special needs, children's playschemes and teaching. While all projects are community-based initiatives that would not be possible without volunteer action, the focus is as much on the aspect of intercultural exchange - both within the group and the local community - as on the work itself.

Projects last for 2-4 weeks with the main season from June to September and smaller winter/spring programme. Volunteers pay a project fee of £115/£125, host organisation fee £80-£200, payable on arrival, preparation weekend fee £25 + travel costs, and fund their own travel and associated expenses. Board and accommodation is free of charge. Concordia also recruits volunteers (20+) to act as Group Co-ordinators on UK based projects, for which training is provided and all expenses are paid. Generally the work doesn't require specific skills or experience, though real motivation and commitment to the project are a must. Concordia currently places volunteers on projects throughout **Western, Eastern and Central Europe, North America, Japan, South Korea and North Africa** on our standard programme and Africa, Asia and Latin America on our North/South programme.

In 2004 Concordia started operating an **MTV (Medium Term Volunteering)** programme. MTV projects usually last between 1 and 6 months (occasionally projects are available for up to 12 months, depending on experience) and take place with certain of our partner organisations in **Europe, Asia, North America, Central America** and **Africa**. MTV projects tend to be individual rather than group based. They include office placements - each year there are placements available to help in the office of our (mainly European) partner organisations during the busy summer season. Our project placements are hosted by local community-based organisations. The range of projects is similar to that on our short-term programme. For further information see website.

In January 2005, Concordia will be offering longer term, funded volunteering opportunities through the European Voluntary Service Programme. Young people aged 18-25 will be able to volunteer in Europe for a period of 6 to 12 months. The type of placement varies from conservation work to social work but most importantly reflects the young person's interests or experience. The Programme will initially be open to volunteers living in S E England.

Crusaders

Kestin House, 45 Crescent Road, Luton, Beds LU2 OAH
Tel: 01582 589850
Email: crusoe@crusaders.org.uk   Web:www.crusaders.org.uk

Crusaders is a non-profit making, interdenominational evangelical Christian youth organisation that runs youth groups for over 19,000 children and young people across the UK. It organises a wide range of activities and adventure holidays for young people in Britain and Europe, with opportunities for volunteers aged 17 upwards. The CRUSOE scheme offers 14-16year olds placements lasting two weeks in a *European country* (Euro Crusoe) and for 16-20 year olds four week placements o*utside Europe* (World Crusoe). Volunteers need to raise funds for their trip (£600 for Europe and £1,500 for World Crusoe). Crusoe Gap is not running during 2004-05. Teams of 10 volunteers with adult leaders work alongside Christians of the placement country, helping with Bible Clubs, evangelistic outreach, building, decorating and gardening work and activities in schools.

do-it.org.uk

Web: www.do-it.org.uk

An online database for UK volunteering opportunities: search by town and activity. The site also includes some international volunteering opportunities.

Eco Africa Experience

Guardian House, Borough Road, Godalming, Surrey, GU7 2AE.
Tel: 01483 860560   Fax: 01483 860391
Email: via website   Web: www.ecoafricaexperience.com

Thinking about a gap year abroad? Consider a unique and exciting gap year in Africa with Eco Africa Experience. We offer you the opportunity to work as a conservation volunteer on some of *Southern Africa*'s premier private game reserves and leading marine ocean research projects. Gap year conservation projects are life changing and highly rewarding. Choose to work on projects such as anti poaching patrols, darting and animal capture, bush rehabilitation or day to day maintenance of the reserve. You can also divide your time by volunteering at different reserves. Our conservation volunteer programmes range from 2 to 12 weeks, so whatever your timeframe, we'll find the ideal placement for you. Sample project cost (Sanbona Wildlife Reserve) 4 weeks: approximately £2,500. 12 weeks: approximately £4,145. This includes
• All Flights (Economy) and Transfers (Airport to reserves)
• All accommodation for duration of stay (Double room, sharing basis)
• All Meals on reserves. Please note the ORCA Foundation is on a half board basis (Breakfast and Lunch)

EIL: Experiment in International Living

287 Worcester Road, Malvern WR14 1AB
Tel: 0800 018 4015   Fax: 01684 562212
Email: info@eiluk.org   Web: www.eiluk.org

Our organisation offers a variety of opportunities for young people 18 to 26 in their gap year. EIL specialises in programmes that bring people of different nationalities together. We can offer programmes from five weeks to a year in length. You can travel out especially for the programme or take time out from part of your trip around the world. There are a selection of project themes; environmental, social care, education, sport and leisure etc. With partner offices in over 25 countries, there is bound to be something for you. Examples are: The *European* Voluntary Service programme (EVS) - volunteer projects ranging from 3 to 12 months. A range of opportunities in the *USA* including College Programmes, Internships, Farmstays and Work and Travel programmes. Ecology & Community Work programmes in *Costa Rica* and the Group Community Service Programme in *Nigeria* can be tailor-made for groups. The Community Service Programme in *India* is for people who would like to spend time learning about India and its people. It includes a homestay with local families. Spanish language programmes are available in *Spain* and *Latin America*.

English Speaking Union Exchange scheme

Dartmouth House, 37 Charles Street, London W1J 5ED
Tel: 020 7529 1550   Fax: 020 7495 6108
Email: esu@esu.org   Web: www.esu.org

The ESU Secondary Schools Exchange scholarships were created in 1928 to promote Anglo-American understanding for the future. Each year 25-30 students in the UK from all backgrounds are offered the opportunity to spend two or three terms at a private school in the *USA or Canada*. The scholarship covers the cost of tuition, board and lodging. All other costs must be covered by the scholar. Students must have taken A-levels or the equivalent and be intending to study at a UK university on their return. They should be under 19 years 6 months old when they take up the scholarship. Although students are placed in a private school in the US, successful applicants come from both the private and maintained sectors in the UK.

European Voluntary Service

Connect Youth, British Council, 10 Spring Gardens, London SW1A 2BN
Tel: 020 7389 4030   Fax: 020 7389 4033
Email:connectyouth.enquiries@britishcouncil.org
Web: www.connectyouthinternational.com

The European Voluntary Service programme, which is funded by the European

Commission, gives people aged between 18 and 25 the opportunity to work as a volunteer in another *European member state*. You might work with children, young people, the elderly, homeless or people with disabilities. Alternatively, you might be involved in environmental projects or help with arts initiatives with minority communities. The programme provides preparation, language training, free board and lodging, pocket money, personal support and in-service training. EVS is unique in that all costs are covered, there is no financial contribution required from the volunteer. For volunteers who wish to volunteer for between 6-12 months there is Long Term EVS. For those who are not ready to spend so long overseas, a first experience of travel and international volunteering is possible with Short Term EVS. For initial details contact the above address.

Experience MexECO

38 Award Road, Fleet, Hampshire GU52 6HG
Tel: 07812 170392 24hour answer service: 01252 629411
Email: info@experiencemexeco.com   Web: www.experiencemexeco.com

Experience MexECO is a company which aims to support conservation and community projects in *Mexico*. Having originally been formed to provide support for sea turtle conservation projects, the need soon became apparent for help within other areas of the community. We now offer our volunteers a unique opportunity to contribute towards a diversity of worthwhile projects, whilst experiencing the excitement and adventure of such a vibrant country and its long-lived traditions. The shortest stay we offer is a period of one month, which allows time to learn the work involved and make a significant contribution towards your project. For those that have more time, two or three months are recommended. Sample prices are as follows: Sea Turtle Conservation £649 (1 month), £1599 (3 months). Prices include: Food, Accommodation, Full staff support, All necessary training. Prices do not include: Flights/ Travel costs to Mexico, Travel insurance, Medical insurance.

French Encounters

63 Fordhouse Road, Bromsgrove, Worcestershire B60 2LU
Tel: 01527 873645   Fax: 01527 832794
Email: admin@frenchencounters.freeserve.co.uk
Web: www.frenchencounters.co.uk

This is a small, independent enterprise running study field trips for 10 to 13 year olds, based in two chateaux in *Normandy*. It employs young people aged 18 to 22 to work for 4 months each year from mid-February as animateurs/ trices. Work involves accompanying coaches and giving commentaries on places visited; supervising children on visits and picnics; organising activities and entertainment. Animateurs' principal role is to encourage children to speak French, enjoy French food and culture and, in the words of the Director,

Patsy Musto, 'become good and positive Europeans'. Applicants need to have good, conversational French. An A level in French is desirable, but students without formal French qualifications will be considered if they have fluency and accuracy. Experience of working with 10 to 13 year-old children would be very useful. The organisation finds that they have plenty of girls applying, but not nearly enough boys, so would particularly welcome enquiries from them. All animateurs who have worked with French Encounters have found the experience invaluable and also hugely enjoyable. They have gained in maturity, organisational and managerial skills and, most important, have improved their linguistic skills immensely. Many have returned in later years to visit, just for fun. All transport, insurance and full board and lodging is provided plus substantial pocket money. Compulsory training and debriefing is also included. Apply before end of August. Interviews are held early to mid September.For further information and application form see new website.

GAP Activity Projects (GAP) Limited

GAP House, 44 Queen's Road, Reading, Berkshire RG1 4BB
Tel: 0118 959 4914   **Fax: 0118 957 6634**
Email:Volunteer@gap.org.uk   **Web:www.gap.org.uk**

GAP arranges voluntary work opportunities overseas for 17 to 19 year olds in their year out between school/college and higher education, employment or training. GAP currently arranges over 1,000 placements annually in 27 countries for volunteers from the UK and 750 placements in the UK for overseas volunteers. Currently opportunities exist in *Argentina, Australia, Brazil, Canada, Chile, China, Costa Rica, Ecuador, Falklands, Fiji, Germany, Ghana, India, Japan, Malawi, Malaysia, Mexico, Nepal, New Zealand, Paraguay, Russia, South Africa, Tanzania, USA, Vietnam, Thailand* and *Vanuatu*. Placements last for between four and eleven months and include assisting with the teaching of English as a Foreign Language, general duties in schools, working with the disadvantaged or people with disabilities, medical work, conservation work and outdoor education projects. Our brochure is published annually in June/July for departures from September of the following year. Copies are available in most schools or colleges and students can also contact the GAP office directly to receive an individual copy. Costs range from £1200 to £1600. This figure includes the GAP Fee, any courses you may require for your placement (for example, Teaching Skills Course, Language Skills or Orientation Course), visa and insurance costs. It does not include any travel costs or additional spending money but does take into account your living allowance (where appropriate).

Students can apply to GAP at any time from the beginning of their final year at school or college, the earlier the better in order to secure the placement and country of their choice. GAP interviews every candidate and has no closing date.As an exchange organisation GAP also brings young people from overseas

95

to undertake voluntary work in the UK - as general assistants or language assistants in schools, in caring organisations and in outdoor activity centres. Check website for brochure and online application form.

Gap Sports Abroad

Willowbank House, 84 Station Road, Bucks SL7 1NX
Tel: 0870 837 9797
Email: info@gapsportsabroad.co.uk   Web: www.gapsportsabroad.co.uk

GAP SPORTS is a specialist organisation that offers a number of unique sports opportunities for adventurous people overseas. These include sports coaching and outreach projects in Africa and Latin America, top-level ski/snowboard instructor courses and adventure training in Canada, and professional sports development programmes at international golf, rugby, cricket, football and scuba academies. No previous experience is needed and we welcome applicants from all walks of life, including gap year takers, undergraduates, postgraduates and career breakers. And with a number of internationally recognised qualifications on offer, you can gain the skills and certifications needed to enter a new career path. Alternatively, GAP SPORTS will give you the chance to share and play the sports you love with others from around the world.

Global Adventures Project

38 Queen's Gate, London SW7 5HR
Freephone: 0800 0854197
Email: info@globaladventures.co.uk   Web: www.globaladventures.co.uk

Global Adventures Project is a gap year programme recently been launched by the American Institute for Foreign Study, the same organisation that runs the well-established Camp America programme.

This new 3 to 12 month programme combines a round-the-world ticket with prearranged placements in both developing and developed countries. In addition to the more traditional voluntary work, you will also get the option to take a language course in universities in Europe as well as the opportunity to earn money along the way. With up to ten stops on your flight ticket, you will be able to travel independently between placements. You choose up to four core options from a choice in Brazil, South Africa, Australia, New Zealand, USA, India and Europe and combine it with your round-the-world ticket to ensure that you really do visit the places you've always dreamed of. The programme adds some structure, a lot of support and a tremendous amount of flexibility.

Greenforce

11-15 Betterton Street, Covent Garden, London WC2H 9BP
Tel:0870 7702646   Fax: 0870 7702647
Email: Greenforce@btinternet.com   Web: www.greenforce.com

INDEPENDENCE DAY

The day you take off on your gap adventure could be your first taste of real freedom. Ideally, you want to pay your own way as much as possible. Open yourself to worthwhile new experiences. Learn stuff – maybe even a new language. A spot of independent travel to places you've always wanted to see. Above all, the flexibility to do whatever you want.

The Global Adventures Project gap year programme gives you all this and more. With voluntary schemes, work placements and study programmes on five continents to choose from, and unlimited scope for independent travel in between, you can pack every day with varied and deeply enriching experiences.

And when you're dealing with people who've organised cultural exchange programmes abroad for over 1 million young people since 1964, you're supported every step of the way. You get:

- **1:1 consultation to select the right programme for you**
- **pre-departure 2 day orientation**
- **round-the-world air ticket with up to 10 stops**
- **24-hour emergency back-up and support**
- **City & Guilds accreditation**

Whether you go for 3 months, 6 months or the full year, it adds up to independence with total security – and an adventure you'll never forget. **Make the most of it.**

This organisation was set up in the wake of the 1992 Rio Earth Summit. It offers environmental assistance to developing countries in order to safeguard the biodiversity of threatened ecosystems. This is done through long term biodiversity and impact surveys, led by experienced scientists and assisted by volunteer Fieldwork Assistants. One aim is to develop conservation enthusiasts by giving these assistants valuable training and the chance to follow up particular interests. These surveys provide vital information to local environmental authorities who otherwise would not be able to afford to carry out this research. Greenforce is invited to do this research and works very closely with the host government. Currently there are terrestrial projects in the *Amazon* and *Zambia* and marine expeditions to reefs in the *Bahamas, Borneo* and *Fiji*.

Volunteers join their chosen projects for ten weeks and there are four start dates in the year. They are trained and supervised by qualified scientists both in residential weekends in the UK and in the host country. Experienced expedition leaders ensure safety which is paramount. For marine expeditions full diver training is provided. The work is funded from the volunteers' contributions, currently £2550. This covers a fund raising guide, training, orientation, food, accommodation etc. In addition you will need to pay for flights to the capital city, an expedition kit and spending money. Further details and application form on the Web. Greenforce holds monthly information evenings at its London office.

Holidaybreak plc

Hartford Manor, Greenbank Lane, Hartford, Cheshire CW8 1HW
Tel: 01606 787522
Email: via website   **Web:www.holidaybreakjobs.com**

Holidaybreak plc (incorporating Eurocamp and Keycamp) is one of Europe's leading tour operators and the market leader in self-driving camping and mobile home holidays, operating in 10 countries throughout *Europe* on over 230 parks and sites. They offer vacancies for couriers on a seasonal contract of up to six months, starting in March/April. Applicants must be over 18. Training is provided for all positions. Campsite couriers carry out a variety of tasks from cleaning accommodation to acting as interpreter.

You will need previous customer service experience and knowledge of a major European language is preferable. Montage/Demontage Assistants: There are a number of posts available for strong and energetic people to set up and take down tents and prepare mobile homes before and after the season. Previous teamwork experience is desirable and you will need experience of previous physical work. Other positions: Applicants with previous team leadership experience and a good working knowledge of a major European language may be employed as a Senior Courier and Courier-in-charge

i-to-i UK

Woodside House, 261 Low Lane, Leeds LS18 5NY
Tel: 0870 333 2332   Fax: 0113 205 4619
Email: uk@i-to-i.com   Web: www.i-to-i.com

i-to-i are a leading volunteer travel organisation specialising in TEFL (Teaching English as a Foreign Language) and Latin American Spanish training for travellers. i-to-i are well-established in this field, providing worthwhile opportunities for travellers since 1994. Currently around 2000 people aged 18+ go on an i-Venture every year to immerse themselves in a new culture. You could: Teach English as a Foreign Language, work in conservation, care work, community development, the media, construction; in *24 countries across Latin America, Africa, Asia, Australia* and *Europe*. i-to-i aim to be as flexible as possible and you can choose from a wide range of start dates, and even do a combination of projects; either in the same country or more than one. All i-Ventures include comprehensive insurance, pre-departure briefing, airport pick-up (except Australia), 24-hour UK support, in-country support from co-ordinators and representatives, orientation sessions, and most include food and accommodation. On some placements it is vital you know the local language. On others it is preferable. And on many you will be fine with English. In Latin American countries, in particular, it is useful to know the language and i-to-i can help you learn with our language add-ons in some destinations. All teaching and community development also provide TEFL training at no extra charge. i-to-i also run intensive weekend TEFL courses all across the UK. Cost for a weekend from £245. See www.weekendtefl.com for details. There is also an online version of the course, available anywhere where there is an internet connection, from the same price of £245. See www.onlineTEFL.com for details.

Extra Training Services include Spanish Courses, which cost just £245 and take place in London and Leeds over weekends throughout the year (see www.weekendspanish.com). Also Travel Photography, Travel Writing and volunteering qualifications. See www.i-to-i.com for details. Sample current project costs (all excluding travel): 4 weeks Conservation in Australia is £795; Journalism in Ireland is £1795 for 8 weeks; community work in Bangalore for 3 weeks is £995; 4 weeks Teaching in Rural Schools in Costa Rica is £1275; 1 week Marine Turtle Conservation in Costa Rica is £675. No qualifications are required to travel with i-to-i.

Intercultural Programmes UK

AFS International, Leeming House, Vicar Lane, Leeds LS2 7JF
Tel: 0113 2426136   Fax: 0113 2430631
Email: info-unitedkingdom@afs.org   Web: www.afsuk.org

AFS is an international, voluntary, non-governmental, non-profit organisation that has provided intercultural learning opportunities since

1947. Its mission is to try to create a more just and peaceful world .There are two main schemes: a Year Programme for 16 to 18 year-olds wishing to spend a year living in a family and going to a local school; and the International Volunteer Programme, more relevant to gap year students . Through the latter scheme young people spend six months in **Brasil, Costa Rica, Guatemala, Honduras, Panama, Peru, Ecuador, Ghana** or **South Africa** living with a local family and working on a local community project. Participants have the opportunity to explore social issues, gain intercultural understanding, learn Spanish or Portuguese and gain in personal skills such as maturity, independence and tolerance. Projects include working with street children, providing them with shelter and teaching them skills, and working on community development projects. Age limits are 18 to 34. Departure dates vary but the fee for participating is the same for each country and is £2950, which includes the cost of intensive language training during the first month. Training is provided and advice is given on fundraising. Full details and a preliminary application form are available from the above address.

International Voluntary Service

IVS South, Old Hall, East Bergholt, Nr Colchester, Essex CO7 6TQ
Tel: 01206 298215   Fax: 01206 299043
Email: ivssouth@ivs-gb.org.uk
IVS North, Castlehill House, 21 Otley Road, Leeds LS6 3AA
Tel: 0113 246 9900   Fax: 0113 246 9910
Email: ivsnorth@ivs-gb.org.uk
IVS Scotland, 7 Upper Bow, Edinburgh EH1 2JN
Tel: 0131 2266722   Fax: 0131 2266723
Email:ivs@ivsgbscot.demon.co.uk
IVS Web: www.ivs-gb.org.uk

IVS is the British branch of Service Civil International and was founded in 1931. It exists to provide opportunities for voluntary work in the belief that this will further international understanding and lead to a more just and peaceful world. IVS organises international voluntary projects in **Europe, North America, Asia, Africa, Latin America** and **Australia** (40 countries in all). IVS projects abroad are open to everyone between 18 and 70 years of age. Volunteers applying for projects in the South (Africa, Asia and South America) or the **Balkans** must be over 21 and preferably have already done a short term project in Europe or have similar relevant experience. Projects in the UK are open to young people over 16. Projects last from two to four weeks. Most take place in the summer, although some are in the autumn and spring months. Projects support the communities by providing outside assistance to worthwhile projects and at the same time give individuals the chance to learn new skills and to live and work with people from other countries and backgrounds. The nature of the work varies enormously: it can involve manual work such as painting and decorating, environmental or conservation work, helping children or people with disabilities. Some camps have a study element. Volunteers pay their own fares, but receive free board and lodging. The 2005 edition of the Summer Project Directory is due out in April 2005.

IST Plus

Rosedale House, Rosedale Road, Richmond Surrey TW9 2SZ
Tel: 020 8939 9057   **Fax: 020 8332 7858**
Email: info@istplus.com   **Web: www.istplus.com**

For information about Work & Travel *Australia*, see under CIEE.

Full-time students in the UK at HND level or above are eligible to apply to the Work & Travel *USA* programme - i.e. gap year/final year students are currently (2005) not eligible.

Work & Travel New Zealand allows you to visit *New Zealand* for a year, taking casual employment as you go and to maximise your job search by using our partner organisation's resource centre and job search facilities. For 18 - 30 year olds.

Japan Exchange and Teaching (JET) Programme

JET Desk, Embassy of Japan, 101-104 Piccadilly, London W1J 7JT
Tel: 020 7465 6668/6670
Email: jet@embjapan.org.uk   **Web: www.jet-uk.org**

Applicants must be graduates so the scheme is suitable for those students wishing to take a gap year (or more) after university. The JET Programme is an official Japanese government scheme to improve foreign language teaching in schools and to promote international understanding. It was set up in 1987 and currently employs several thousand graduates from 41 different countries. UK graduates are mainly recruited as Assistant Language Teachers (ALTs) to help teach Japanese children aged 12 upwards in one or more schools in a particular area. Various locations in cities, towns and villages throughout *Japan* are available and applicants can specify preferences, though these are not guaranteed. ALTs team-teach or assist Japanese Teachers of English, assist in the preparation of teaching materials and participate in extra-curricular activities with pupils. A TEFL qualification is useful but not essential. Applicants with good written and spoken Japanese can apply to work as Co-ordinators for International Relations, assisting in local government offices with international activities at a local level. The contract is for a minimum of one year, but is renewable for up to two years. ALTs work a 35 hour week, Monday to Friday. Salary is 3,600,000 yen after Japanese taxes. (Sufficient for all normal expenses, including rent and compulsory Japanese N.I. payments.) Return air travel is provided. The host institution helps with finding accommodation. Application forms and information are available to download from the website: and you can apply online at this web address too.

Jobs in the Alps

Email: info@jobs-in-the-alps.co.uk   Web: www.jobs-in-the-alps.com

Website for student jobs in ski resorts - Winter and Summer seasons. We have a large variety of jobs to place, most with *European* Hotels and Restaurants. Each year we place some 250 people. In winter many candidates are Gap-Year or recently Graduated. In summer a job may be to help with a University Course, keep language skills up to date or just give you a chance to be away in the mountains. Majority of jobs rely on some language abilities, others are available for non speakers. These Jobs In The Alps earn you a decent salary, give generous time off, look good on a CV and are a great experience.

Junior Language Assistants Scheme

British Council Language Assistants Team, Education and Training Group, British Council, 10 Spring Gardens, London SW1A 2BN
Tel: 020 7389 4596
Email assistants@britishcouncil.org
Web: www.britishcouncil.org/education

This scheme allows people aged 18 to 20, with an A level or equivalent in German , to spend an academic year working in a boarding school in *Germany*. Board, lodging and monthly allowance provided. The number of posts is limited and competition very strong. The schools tend to be located in small towns or isolated country districts, often with limited public transport facilities. You will be working under the guidance of the English teaching staff and will be frequently required to supervise and help pupils do their English homework and to give extra tuition to individual pupils where necessary. You may be asked to take small groups of pupils for English conversation and to give them an insight into British life, customs and institutions. Applications should be in by 31 March. Contact the Assistants Team or apply online from website.

Kibbutz Representatives

1A Accommodation Road, London NW11 8ED
Tel: 020 8458 9235   Fax: 020 8455 7930
Email:enquiries@kibbutz.org.uk

A Kibbutz is a rural, communal settlement in which work, income and property are shared by its members. Kibbutz members generally work within their community, in agriculture, industry and the service areas (kitchen, laundry, dining-room etc). When too few members are available for a particular job, the Kibbutz takes in volunteers who live on the Kibbutz and share in the work and Kibbutz lifestyle in *Israel*. Kibbutz Representatives is the organisation responsible for representing the Kibbutz movement outside Israel. They will be pleased to supply information about Kibbutzim and help you enjoy a wonderful holiday on a Kibbutz. For more information contact their UK office.

Latin Link STEP Programmes and STRIDE Placements

175 Tower Bridge Road, London SE1 2AB
Tel: 020 7939 9000   Fax: 020 7939 9015
Email: step.uk@latinlink.org or   stride.uk@latinlink.org
Web: www.stepteams.org or   www.latinlink.org

Latin Link is a Christian missionary agency with many years of experience working with evangelical churches in Latin America. STEP (Short-Term Experience Projects) enables people to live and work alongside a Latin American church community whilst helping in a basic building project. Previous years' projects have included helping to build orphanages, street kids' shelters, classrooms and community centres in six countries. Teams also help churches with evangelism, working with young people, music, drama and even preaching. Teams go and work in *Argentina, Bolivia, Brazil, Cuba, Ecuador, Mexico* and *Peru*, or most recently in *Spain* and *Portugal*. Summer projects in these countries run for seven weeks, from mid-July to early September. Spring projects run for four months from March to July. 'Steppers' are aged 17 upwards. Contribution for Spring Project only is £ 2,450. There is also a Senior Step team that goes for four weeks and is for over 35's only.

STRIDE placements are for applicants aged 18 years and over and last between 6 months and 2 years. Participants work in placements tailored to their skills. They usually live with a Latin American family and are linked to a support team. Placements have included children's work, teaching, church planting, and farming. Applicants for both programmes must be committed Christians. Knowledge of Spanish or Portuguese is not essential but is extremely advantageous and applicants are advised to take at least a basic language course. Applications for STEP should be made approximately six months before departure to the STEP Coordinator at the above address. Enquiries about STRIDE should be directed to the Special Programmes Coordinator.

The Leap

The Leap Overseas Ltd, 1st Floor, 121 - 122 High Street, Marlborough, Wiltshire SN8 1NZ
Tel: 0870 240 4187   Fax: 01488 71311
Email: info@theleap.co.uk   Web: www.theleap.co.uk

The Leap is a company dedicated to the Gap Year industry, providing British students aged over eighteen and employees taking career sabbaticals with the opportunity to carry out work placements in some of the most exclusive and coveted destinations in the World.

We specialise in overseas voluntary work placements focused on eco-tourism, combined with a strong emphasis on conservation & community issues. All placements are in bush camps, safari lodges, private ranches and boutique hotels, in game parks, bush reserves, conservation & coastal locations. Destinations are in **Kenya, Tanzania, Malawi, Botswana, South Africa** and **Zambia.** Volunteers are involved in a variety of activities including management, operations, hospitality, catering & maintenance as well as involvement with community & conservation projects, such as assisting in eco-tourism & conservation for the protection, survival and management of wildlife, tribal people & environments. They will also be helping the professionals provide activities such as: game walks, horse and camel safaris, deep-sea fishing etc.

Placements are voluntary/non paid. On some placements (Safari Camps) the volunteers receive a local living allowance. The cost for Safari Camp Placements is £2100 - £2200, including Familiarisation and Selection Course, 24 hour emergency back-up and support, Insurance, Living allowance, Airport pick up and transfer to and from the placement, Full board and accommodation. Flights, visas and independent travel are not included. Prices vary for Conservation and Community Placements and Working Farms and Game Ranch Placements. We need individuals who are committed, enthusiastic and motivated, who work well in a team and are prepared to get stuck in.

Madventurer

Madventurer HQ, Hawthorn House, Forth Banks, Newcastle NE1 3SG
Tel: 0845 121 1996
Email: team@madventurer.com   Web: www.madventurer.com

Madventurer combine Award Winning Development Projects and Adventurous Overland Travel to offer those taking a gap year, university students, and career-breakers a unique experience. You can join us for 2 weeks or 5 weeks on a project and then undertake an Adventure that runs from 3 weeks to 3 months. You can also choose to combine two 5 week projects in any Madventurer destination.

Projects in **Ghana, Togo, Trinidad & Tobago, Kenya, Tanzania, Uganda, Peru, Tonga** and **Fiji.** Projects are flexible and allow experience to be gained in more than one discipline, e.g. teaching, building, sports coaching, medicine, conservation, tourism, architecture, carework, physiotherapy and professional disciplines. Love Sport? Why not stop off on your gap year out to coach and play cricket, football or rugby in the exotic locations of **Fiji, Tonga, Ghana,** or **Trinidad & Tobago**. For more information on our specialist sports programmes visit www.sportventurer.com

The organisation's ethos is 'developing together'. Our aim is to assist rural community development whilst at the same time enabling adventurous travellers to gain experience through the interaction with local people. Sample costs: 2 weeks project only in Kenya £750, project plus 32 day adventure £1,180. 5 weeks project only in **Kenya, Tanzania** or **Uganda** £1,480, project plus 32 day adventure £1,910.

The Mission to Seafarers

St Michael Paternoster Royal, College Hill, London EC4R 2RL
Tel: 020 7248 5202   Fax: 020 7248 4761
Email: ministry@missiontoseafarers.org   Web: www.missiontoseafarers.org

Candidates aged 21 to 26, Christian, can be accepted for one year helping to run clubs and recreational facilities, ship and hospital visiting, and assisting the Chaplain. The gap year scheme is open to those looking to gain wider experience through service to others before taking up work or furthering their education. It may be of particular interest to those who are thinking of full-time ministry in the church and who want to undertake a practical Christian mission. These are some of the ports where chaplain's assistants have been placed in recent years: **Auckland, Dunkerque, Immingham, Kobe, Liverpool, Mombasa, Rotterdam, Seaham, Singapore, Southampton** and **Yokohama**. Candidates should have a valid driving licence. Travel costs, board and lodging and pocket money provided. Contact the Ministry Secretary.

Outreach International

Bartlett's Farm, Hayes Road, Compton Dundon, Somerset TA11 6PF
Tel or Fax: 01458 274957
Email: projects@outreachinternational.co.uk
Web: www.outreachinternational.co.uk

Outreach International was established to bridge the gap between the growing interest amongst young people with a thirst for adventure and a desire to work overseas with the urgent need for assisting grass root projects in developing countries. We offer a range of gap year projects of 3 to 9 months duration in **Mexico, Ecuador** and **Cambodia**. Projects for 2004 – 2005 include: Environmental & Conservation, Community Development, Teaching & Education, Humanitarian Aid Work, Orphanages & Street Children.

Mexico   This is a vibrant country and offers the chance to experience the richness of culture and geography while participating in an environmental, medical, educational, social or arts project. More specifically these include: Turtle Conservation, Crocodile Protection, Open Air Whale Watching, Eco-tourism Expeditions Project, Dolphin Training Project, Special Needs School, School for Deaf Children, Orphanage and Disabled Children Project, Street Children Project, Library, Teaching and Community Development project in a Pacific coast village, Teaching Projects, Dance Project.

Cambodia   This beautiful country needs volunteers to work as English and games teachers and also to work at rehabilitation centres for landmine victims, to work with street children and to work on art and craft projects.

In Ecuador volunteers have been asked to assist with reforestation and conservation schemes in the Amazon rainforest, help on a street children and orphanage project, and also help at a medical centre for children.

In Mexico we offer an intensive one week course to volunteers on arrival. The course is run by a specialist Spanish tutor who uses accelerated learning techniques. In Ecuador, on arrival volunteers attend a two week intensive Spanish course. During these two weeks volunteers stay with a Ecuadorian family. In Cambodia Khmer lessons and a cultural orientation are provided for the first week by a private tutor.

Sample project cost (Mexico) is £3250 for three months and then £450 a month for each subsequent month. This includes all air transport, food, accommodation, training, insurance and full in-country support.

Overseas Working Holidays

Level 1, 51 Fife Rd, Kingston, Surrey KT1 1SFY
Tel: 0845 344 0366
Email: via website   Web: www.overseasworkingholidays.co.uk

Your gap year is a fantastic opportunity to experience different cultures, meet new friends and if you choose, even earn some money to supplement your travels. Whether your dream is to be working at the biggest sporting events in Australia, a season in the Canadian resorts, or helping the children or animals of Africa, Overseas Working Holidays can make your dreams a reality through our Working Holidays or our Volunteer Programs.

PGL Travel

Penyard Lane, Ross-on-Wye, Herefordshire HR9 5NR
Tel: 01989 767833
Email: pglpeople@pgl.co.uk   Web: www.pgl.co.uk/personnel

PGL have opportunities for group leaders and instructors to assist in their adventure holidays and courses in **France and Spain** for young people aged 6-18 (also opportunities in the UK). The main activities are canoeing, sailing, windsurfing and pony trekking, plus a wide range of other activities including abseiling, challenge courses and archery. Instructional posts require relevant experience and Group Leaders (who look after the children outside of activity sessions) need experience of working with/looking after children. There is also a range of jobs for inexperienced staff as Site or Catering Assistants, Domestics and Tuck Shop staff. Food and accommodation are provided in addition to a living allowance (in line with the National Minimum Wage). The PGL season lasts from February to November. You can apply to work for this full period, for as little as eight weeks or for any period in between. Some vacancies, including at Southern French and Spanish centres, are for shorter-term contracts. The website includes comprehensive information about UK and international employment opportunities, including online application facilities.

Pod (Personal Overseas Development)

Linden Cottage, The Burgage, Prestbury, Cheltenham GL52 3DJ
Tel: 01242 250 901
Email: info@thepodsite.co.uk   **Web: www.thepodsite.co.uk/**

Gap Year Programmes include:

• One to six month Gap Programmes in the developing world

• Summer Mini-Gaps for school leavers going straight to University

• Voluntary work and placements where you can make a difference

• Adventurous activities, tourist travel and cultural visits

• Fully supported and supervised programmes to ensure high levels of quality and safety

• Remote mountain villages in Africa; tropical islands in SE Asia; ancient Inca capital in South America

Sample prices e.g. for Teaching English for 3 months in Tanzania: £2195 or Wildlife Rescue for 1 - 3 months in Thailand: £710 - £1340. These prices include: training in the UK (for teaching and orphanage placements), training in-country (depending on the role and location), ongoing support, help and advice from our local teams, travel insurance, accommodation. Many of the Programmes also include adventure activities such as a safari in *Tanzania*, learning to scuba dive in *Thailand*, or white water rafting in *Peru*.

The Project Trust

The Hebridean Centre, Isle of Coll, Argyll, Scotland PA78 6TE
Tel: 01879 230444   **Fax: 01879 230357**
Email: info@projecttrust.org.uk   **Web: www.projecttrust.org.uk**

Qualifications required: Must be 17-19 years old and doing A levels, Scottish Highers or equivalent. A full year away! There are 90 projects in 24 countries in *Africa, Asia, Central and South America* and the *Middle East*. Volunteers teach, work in orphanages, with adults, with people with disabilities, instruct outward bound, work in development, do environmental projects and much more. Work includes teaching of all different kinds and to all ages, working with the disabled or under-privileged, medical work, development and environmental projects. Placements are for a full year and training is provided at a purpose built selection and training centre on the Isle of Coll. Project Trust runs seminars and workshops to assist fund-raising the £3,950 required to go overseas. It covers nearly all costs of a year

(11-12 months) overseas, including training, air fares, medical insurance and extensive support. Are you looking for a challenge and adventure? For a lifetime's experience in your gap year, come and talk to us!

Quest Overseas

The North-West Stables, Borde Hill Estate, Balcombe Road, Haywards Heath, West Sussex RH16 1XP
Tel: 01444 474744   **Fax: 01444 474799**
Email: emailingyou@questoverseas.com   Web: www.questoverseas.com

South American Quest lasts 3 months, with 3 weeks of language training, a 4 week project e.g:

- *Brazil*: Rio Kids Carnival/Conservation/Community

- *Peru*: Shanty Town Kids

- *Bolivia*: Animal Sanctuary

- *Ecuador*: Forest Conservation/Amazon Community
  6 weeks Andean Expedition/Brazilian Expedition. Cost approximately £4,500.
  Quest Africa also lasts 3 months, with a 6 week project:

- *Swaziland* Game Reserve Project

- *Tanzania* Community Project

And a 6 week expedition. Cost approximately £4,130 (covers all food, accommodation and activities while in Africa).

Rotary International in Great Britain & Ireland,

Kinwarton Road, Alcester, Warwickshire B49 6PB
Tel: 01789 765411   **Fax: 01789 765570**
Web: www.rotary-ribi.org/4_ctte/international/international.htm

Each year Rotary Youth Exchange provides over 9000 young people *worldwide* the opportunity to see the world as it should be seen by meeting and living with people from other lands and cultures, learning another language and discovering themselves, who they are and of what they are capable but most of all Rotary will be planting in them the seeds of international understanding. Opportunities can vary from a two week camp in Europe through short term home stays, with or without vocational or academic study, to a full year living and studying in another country. Rotary's Youth Exchange programmes are open to the relatives of Rotarians and non-Rotarians alike. The Long Term Exchange is open to students between the ages of 15 and 19 who are above average in their abilities and possess the qualities which will enable them to become excellent cultural ambassadors and who have a willingness to try new things. For further information about programmes and eligibility see the website.

Starfish Ventures Ltd

199 Bishopsgate, London EC2M 3TY
Tel: 020 7814 6641   Fax: 020 7814 6611
Email: enquiries@starfishventures.co.uk   Web: www.starfishventures.co.uk

All of Starfish Ventures projects are in *Thailand* but they are the length and breadth of the country. Starfish Ventures are open to anyone aged between 18 and 55. You do not require any formal qualifications to take part in a Starfish Venture. For Teaching English we provide a condensed Teaching English as a Foreign Language course. All that is required otherwise is enthusiasm and commitment to your chosen Venture! You can choose from ventures such as: teaching English, school development, turtle conservation, dog rescue centre, nursing. The price for Teaching English for 4 weeks is £1095, for 12 weeks £1,495, whilst 4 weeks at the dog rescue centre is £995 and 8 weeks is £1195. This covers TEFL weekend, Insurance , Airport pickup, Airport transfer, Accommodation,24 hour support but not International flight, Visa, Food, Expenses.

Students Partnership Worldwide (SPW)

17 Dean's Yard, London, SW1P 3PB
Tel: 020 7222 0138   Fax: 020 7233 0008
Email: spwuk@gn.apc.org   Web: www.spw.org

Every year thousands of young people from the UK travel to Africa and Asia. For most, their time abroad changes their lives, but does nothing for the millions of local young people who are struggling for survival. Do you want to take a holiday in the world's poorest countries and give nothing back? As an SPW volunteer you will engage with the most important issues affecting young people in rural areas, such as AIDS, soil erosion and clean water. After 4-6 weeks training you can help young people begin to tackle these problems for themselves. Half of our volunteers are recruited from within the countries where we work.

With partners who understand the culture and the problems, you can achieve so much more. It is difficult, but nearly all our volunteers come back saying their time with SPW was incredibly rewarding - and great fun. Every year SPW recruits and trains over 600 volunteers to work on Health education and Community Resource Programmes in rural parts of *India, Nepal, South Africa, Tanzania, Uganda, Zambia* and *Zimbabwe*. We have offices in every country to provide you with comprehensive training, support and advice. We accept volunteers with A level or equivalent qualifications, aged 18-28. The cost is around £2900-£3300. This is all inclusive, covering open return flight, accommodation, basic living allowance, insurance, pre-departure and in-country training and office support.

The Sunseed Trust

Sunseed Desert Technology, Apdo 9, 04270 Sorbas, Almeria, Spain
Tel: (+34) 950 4525 770
Email: sunseedspain@arrakis.es   Web: www.sunseed.org.uk

This organisation is dedicated to research, education and sustainable living. It aims to find and spread new ways to reclaim desert soils and to help the hard lives of people on threatened land. At the same time they try to live 'green' lives. It runs a research centre in *Spain* (in Almeria, which has the driest climate in Europe), called Sunset Desert Technology. Research falls largely into two categories. Our biological section undertakes dryland regeneration and investigates special methods of cultivation. Our appropriate technology work aims to develop lowcost applications which could be used in semi arid areas throughout the world. Every year up to three hundred international volunteers come to work at the centre. Sunseed Desert Technology welcomes students at any level who wish to carry out a placement or project at Sunseed as part of their course.

Full-time volunteers work for 5 weeks or more (working 35 hours a week) either specialising in one section of the work or trying out several. This can be particularly useful for school leavers intending to go on to degrees in environmental sciences, botany, agriculture or similar disciplines. Volunteers arrange their own travel and make a weekly donation which varies slightly according to the time of year. The minimum for a week is around £49 which includes basic accommodation and food. This is very much about low-impact community living, in an isolated area, but there is a range of recreational and social activities.

Syndicat Mixte Montaigu-Rocheserviere 33

35 Avenue Villebois Mareuil, 85607 Montaigu, France
Tel: (0033) 2 51 46 45 45   Fax: (0033) 2 51 46 45 40
Email: julie_legree@yahoo.co.uk   Web: www.explomr.com/english

This is a local government scheme for students with A level French looking for a year's teaching experience in *France*. The scheme is in the Nantes area and has been running for ten years. It is an opportunity for high calibre, mature students who are genuinely interested in French life, culture and the teaching profession. There are four posts in primary school and one in College and Lycee each year. Contracts run from October to May and involve approximately 20 hours a week teaching. Assistants are given free board and lodging with local families and a monthly allowance. Full training, comprising of a two week unpaid intensive period mid-September is provided, with ongoing support throughout the year. Applications close on 31 May. Interviews are held in England in July. Contact Mrs J Legree, resident Project Co-ordinator.

Teaching & Projects Abroad

Teaching & Projects Abroad, Aldsworth Parade, Goring, Sussex BN12 4TX
Tel : 01903 708300   Fax: 01903 501026
Email: info@teaching-abroad.co.uk   Web:www.teaching-abroad.co.uk

Programmes are available in *Bolivia, Chile, China, Ghana, India, Mexico, Mongolia, Nepal, Peru, Romania, Russia, Senegal, Sri Lanka, South Africa, Swaziland, Thailand* and *Togo*. You can also Earn in Australia. You can get involved in Teaching, Care & Community, Medicine, Conservation, Business, Journalism, Veterinary Medicine, Animal Care, Active Learning, Sport, Law, Nomad projects, Inca projects, Archaeology, Spanish & Russian. Nobody is isolated and you can choose your own dates/duration.

Apart from our 2-Week Specials, placements are flexible and most last from one month upwards. Most volunteers go for between two and four months. You can combine placements, both within a country and across countries - see the Combinations section of the website for more details and combination ideas.

Teaching & Projects Abroad programmes cost from £845. Our costs include all food, accommodation, comprehensive travel and medical insurance, and support from our expert staff at home and abroad. We have full-time paid and trained English-speaking staff in each destination. It is their job to set up placements, check out your accommodation, meet you at the airport and provide you with any support you need should any problems occur. Many of our volunteers are between 18 and 25 years old, but volunteers are welcome between the ages of 16 and 75. Non-UK passport holders most welcome.

Travellers

7 Mulberry Close, Ferring, West Sussex BN12 5HY
Tel:/Fax: 01903 502595
Email: info@travellersworldwide.com   Web: www.travellersworldwide.com

Travellers offers volunteers the unique opportunity to teach conversational English (and/or other subjects like maths, music, sport etc) to children and adults in a growing range of less advantaged countries, including *India, Kenya, Guatemala, Brazil, Sri Lanka, Russia, South Africa, Ukraine* and *Malaysia*. No formal qualifications or knowledge of the local language are necessary, although applicants must be very enthusiastic and have a spirit of adventure! You can Coach Sports in some of our destinations and we also have conservation and work experience placements available. The latter include Law, Journalism, Medicine, Architecture, Hotel & Catering, Web Design, Veterinary Medicine and Tourism. You can take Language Courses in *Argentina, Cuba, Guatemala, Russia* and *Ukraine* and Cultural Courses in Argentina and Cuba: Learn the Salsa and Tango in

Argentina, or take Photography, Music, Arts or Drama courses in Cuba. Our programmes are open to all ages and placements are available throughout the year, lasting from 2 weeks to one year. They are extremely flexible and are tailored to suit your choice and your needs. These programmes benefit both our volunteers and the local community and are enjoyed by all. Sample charges for 3 months teaching are: India £1,395, Sri Lanka £1,495, Russia £1,495, Kenya £1,575. These placements include all your food and accommodation, as well as transport from the airport to your school. We can also arrange international flights to and from your destination country.

UNA-Exchange

Temple of Peace, Cathays Park, Cardiff CF10 3AP
Tel: 029 20223088   **Fax: 029 20665557**
Email: info@unaexchange.org   **Web: www.unaexchange.org**

UNAExchange provides opportunities to participate in International Volunteer Projects in *Europe, North Africa, North America, Japan* and *South Korea* (main programme) and in *Africa, South and South East Asia* and *Latin America* (North South Programme). Before applying for projects on the latter Programme you need to come to an North South Orientation in Cardiff. There are also opportunities to get involved in leading projects in Wales with groups of international volunteers.

The majority of the projects last between two and four weeks and involve either environmental, construction or basic social work. As long as you can find projects which fit together you can apply for as many projects in as many countries as you like. You will need to pay a placement fee for each project. Medium Term Volunteering projects are available in Europe, Mexico, Thailand and Kenya. These are individual placements for volunteers working for 1 to 12 months.

Volunteers meet their own travelling and insurance costs in addition to the placement fee. Board and lodging are generally provided for the duration of the project. For more information please contact UNA-exchange at the above address. The organisation is also involved with the European Voluntary Service programme.

Universal Aunts

PO Box 304, London SW4 0NN
Tel: 020 7738 8937   **Web: www.universalaunts.co.uk**

Established in 1921, Universal Aunts provides men and women for short and long term residential work *anywhere in the world*, and short and long term daily work in the London area. Services cover Nannies, Mother's Helps, Proxy Parents, Child Escorts and Babysitters, Housekeeper/companions, Cooks, all domestic situtations. Not an au pair agency. Driving licence useful.

Venture Co Worldwide

The Ironyard, 64 - 66 The Market Place, Warwick. CV34 4SD.
Tel: 01926 411 122   Fax: 001926 411 133.
Email: mail@ventureco-worldwide.com
Web: www.ventureco-worldwide.com

Gap Year and Career Break providers in *South America, Central America, the Himalayas, the Rift Valley* and *Indochina*. Ventures are four-months long and consist of three elements: 1 Learn the language and live the local culture; 2 Volunteer on an aid project; 3 Join an expedition to explore the mountains and back-roads.

Inca Venture:
- 3 weeks spent learning or improving Spanish and cultural orientation, Quito, Ecuador.
- 4 weeks project working with children or in conservation.
- 8 week expedition culminating in the Inca Trail to Machu Picchu

Patagonia Venture:
- 3 weeks spent learning or improving Spanish and cultural orientation, Cusco, Peru.
- 4 weeks conservation project working in the Andes or Amazon rainforest.
- 8 week expedition culminating at the Patagonia Ice Cap.

Aztec-Maya Venture:
- 3 weeks spent learning or improving Spanish in Oaxaca
- 4 weeks conservation project working in Honduras, Belise or Costa Rica.
- 8 week expedition culminating in trekking, mountain biking and white water rafting in Costa Rica.

Himalaya Venture:
- includes cultural orientation in the Delhi area, Rajasthan Vishnois Village Project, expedition culminating in Everest Base Camp Trek.

The Indochina Venture:
- journey through through Cambodia, Vietnam, Loas and China.

The Rift Valley Venture:
- to Kenya, Uganda and Tanzania.

Venturers are selected by interview. Cost (including flights) around £4,595 to 5,435 all inclusive.

Village Education Project (Kilimanjaro)

Mint Cottage, Prospect Road, Sevenoaks, Kent TN13 3UA
Tel: 01732 459799
Email: info@kiliproject.org   Web: www.kiliproject.org

This registered charity was set up in 1994. The overall aim is to improve the education of primary school children by renovating government buildings, providing books and teaching aids and sponsoring in-service teacher training. The gap year Student Project is one of the charity's most recent projects. The students help to teach English in village schools. A pre-departure two week training course is given in Sevenoaks, Kent, but students are encouraged to provide extra-curricular activities such as sport, art and music for their pupils, who are between 7 and 14 years old. The students accompany parties of children on school outings to a National Park and to the coast.

Students live in their own village house, and their life in the village involves lots of walking each day up and down the lush countryside of *Kilimanjaro*'s slopes. School holidays provide an opportunity for further travel - *Zanzibar* being a favourite destination. Katy Allen MBE, the project leader, lived in Kilimanjaro for three years and now visits the region for at least four months each year. She is there to meet the gap year students and help them settle into their village and their schools, giving advice and guidance. They have at all times the full support of the local community and church and, specifically, of the ex-head of a local school now seconded to work for the charity.

The cost of £2500 (subject to change) includes the return flight, village accommodation, pre-departure training (including teaching methodology and essential Kiswahili) and most teaching materials. Students have to pay their own living costs and insurance. Details of placements and beyond are available from the above address. Details and application form can be downloaded from the website.

VSO (Voluntary Service Overseas)

317 Putney Bridge Road, London SW15 2PN
Tel: 020 8780 7500   Fax: 020 9780 7300
Email: enquiry@vso.org.uk   Web: www.vso.org.uk

VSO standard programme offers opportunities for qualified and experienced profesisonals to work overseas as teachers, trainers and advisers, on two year placements. However, they also run two youth programmes that may be suitable for a GAP year:

THE WORLD YOUTH PROGRAMME is a six-month international exchange scheme for people ages 17-25. It's a unique opportunity to live and work alongside young people from a developing country. You would make a practical contribution where it is most needed, develop and share skills and promote international understanding. The scheme lasts six months, with volunteers working for three months in the UK and three months in the exchange country. The programme is structured around five 'core components' that are the same for the UK and the overseas phase of the programme.

They are: counterpart pairs, host communities, host families, work placements and educational activity days.

The YOUTH FOR DEVELOPMENT PROGRAMME is aimed at young people, aged between 18 and 25 who live in the UK or Ireland, with at least one year volunteering experience and/or community work. Placements are for 10 to 12 months. VSO country programmes support local initiatives which address the causes and symptoms of disadvantage. Examples of YfD placements include initiatives in Education, HIV and AIDS, Disability, Health and Social Well-being, Secure livelihoods and Participation and Governance.

All costs are paid, but participants on both schemes are expected to raise £600 from their community.

Winant-Clayton Volunteer Association

St Margaret's House, 21 Old Ford Road, Bethnal Green, London. E2 9PL
Tel: 020 8 983 3834
Email: wcva@dircon.co.uk   Web: www.wcva.dircon.co.uk

This is an exchange scheme for voluntary community service in the *Eastern States of America*. We are looking for volunteers from all backgrounds from the ages of 18 to 80. Previous experience of voluntary work is valuable but by no means essential. Volunteers should have a real interest in people, a sense of humour and stamina! Work is with children, adolescents, the elderly, those in need of psychiatric rehabilitation or the homeless. The period is from end-June to mid-September. Whilst working you will receive free accommodation and a stipend living allowance which covers your basic expenses such as food and travel.

Volunteers pay for flight, insurance and own travel expenses during the last two weeks. Placements last for eight weeks. At the end of your placements you will have roughly 2-3 weeks for travelling. There is a hospitality list of people you can stay with around the country. Only open to UK citizens. Send s.a.e. for details to the Coordinator. Applications by end of January. Forms available from September onwards.

WorldNetUK

Emberton House, 26 Shakespeare Road, Bedford MK40 2ED
Tel: 0845 458 1551
Email:info@worldnetuk.com   Web: www.worldnetuk.com

WorldNetUK is a leading work and travel company offering opportunities for young people to work and travel overseas. We offer:Camp *USA*; Childcare and nanny Programme - USA; Study Programme USA; Ski and Summer Resort Nanny - Europe; Childrens' Summer Camp - Italy; Au Pair programmes - UK and Europe. Call for brochure.

Youth Action for Peace

8 Golden Ridge, Freshwater, Isle of Wight PO40 9LE
Tel: 08701 657 927
Email: action@yap-uk.org   **Web: www.yap-uk.org**

YAP is an international movement which works towards a society of justice, peace and human solidarity. The International Secretariat is based in Brussels. YAP organises international youth exchanges, sending volunteers to 'workcamps' in *Europe, Africa, Asia* and the *Americas*. Most projects run from June to September and last 2 to 6 weeks. Work undertaken ranges from manual, for example in conservation, to social work, for example children's play schemes. All aim to support local communities and to encourage young people to be more aware of other cultures. Volunteers normally receive board and lodging, but have to pay their own fares, plus a placement fee and in developing countries a hosting fee. Full details of available projects around the world are listed on the website plus full details of how to apply. Volunteers in the North-South programme (projects in Africa, Asia, Latin America) must attend a North-South Training Weekend prior to departure unless they can convince us that they have sufficient workcamp or related and travel experience. We also ask for a motivation letter from each volunteer.

Joining an expedition

This section is devoted to a selection of organisations that specialise in providing expeditions, exploratory projects in remote locations, and other active pursuits. All require at least average physical fitness, and the ability to withstand being outdoors in all weathers and, sometimes, experiencing fairly basic living conditions.

Conservation expeditions

There is some overlap between this section and Section Five: International Opportunities which lists a number of conservation projects, some of which are described as conservation expeditions.

Working in an active holiday centre

Those organisations which offer gap year employment opportunities for group leaders, instructors and other assistants to assist with active holidays for young people are included in Section Four: UK Opportunities, and Section Five: International Opportunities.

Licensing and inspection

In 1996, the Government established a licensing and inspection scheme for providers who sell adventure activities to schools and to the public. This covers 26 main activities under the broad headings of caving, climbing, trekking and watersports and includes pony trekking and mountain biking. The body responsible for this scheme is the Adventure Activities Licensing Authority (AALA), a non-departmental public authority which holds the official list of licensed providers. Both consumers and those thinking of working in this area would be well advised to check the position of any organisation to which they are considering applying. AALA can be contacted at 17 Lambourne Crescent, Llanishen, Cardiff CF14 5GS by telephone on 02920 755715 or online at www. aala.org. For further information about AALA please see entry in Section Three: Planning Organisations.

Other active holidays

There are a great many activity holiday organisations in addition to those mentioned in this section. Many belong to The British Activity Holiday Association, a self-regulatory trade association formed to maintain high standards, and these are listed together with their activities on the BAHA website: www.baha.org.uk. For further information about BAHA please see entry in Section Three: Planning Organisations.

Sport instructor awards

See entries in Section Seven: Study options.

Army Short Service Volunteer Commission

Tel: 08457 300 111
Web:www.armyofficer.co.uk

Though many use it to 'test the water' before committing themselves to an Army career, the Gap Year Commission (GYC) – a relatively new scheme - is ultimately an opportunity to take a year out and experience something new and exciting. In short, the GYC is a personal development training package with adventure thrown in. Similarly the Undergraduate Army Placement (UGAP) is a year in which you can use the experience of being an Army officer to fulfil the Placement needs of your degree course. Once you join your Regiment and find your feet, your responsibilities will grow and your intellectual agility and personal qualities will be put to the test. You'll broaden your horizons and discover a great deal about yourself and your abilities. You'll develop in every way possible - the ultimate preparation for university and your future career, whatever it may be. Past Gap Year Commission Officers have spent their time trekking and horse-riding in the Rocky Mountains, on a sailing expedition around Norway and Bavaria, white water rafting in Belize and on Exercises in and around Hong Kong.

Selection takes place at the Regular Commissions Board (RCB) at Westbury in Wiltshire. The Board doesn't expect you to have all the attributes of a ready-made Army officer, but will look for your strengths and weaknesses and assess your potential to become an Army officer after training. It lasts three and a half intensive days but you will receive a full briefing beforehand.

Base Camp Group

Unit 30, Baseline Business Studios, Whitchurch Road, London W11 4AT
Tel: 020 7243 6222
Email: contact@basecampgroup.com   Web: www.basecampgroup.com

Base Camp Group's Gap Snowsports Programme is an 11 week intensive programme teaching you to become ski or snowboard instructors. With coaching from ex-Olympians and professional extreme skiers, the instruction from Snow-Systems Ski School is second to none. You are trained and prepared for European accepted BASI (British Association of Snowsport Instructors) qualifications as well as having off-piste, freestyle, freeride, mogul and race training. And all this in the largest ski area in the world. With over 200 lifts, 600 km of groomed runs and 35 000 acres of off-piste, the facilites Meribel and Les 3 Vallees have to offer are unparalleled. As well as food, accommodation, a full season ski pass, and lessons 6 hours a day 5 days a week, also included in the programme are an avalanche and mountain awareness course, a first aid course, ski and snowboard tuning clinics, French lessons and a post programme service finding you work in ski schools. The programme is ideal for anyone on a Gap Year or who is looking to take time out from work.

Brathay Exploration Group

Brathay Hall, Ambleside, Cumbria LA22 OHP
Tel/Fax: 01539 433942
Email: admin@brathayexploration.org.uk
Web:www.brathayexploration.org.uk

This registered charity has been running expeditions and courses for over 50 years. It offers participants each year the chance to explore remote areas of the UK, mainly Scotland, and a varied range of foreign destinations such as Ireland, mainland Europe, Africa, Asia and the Far East. Expedition leaders are all volunteers, many of whom trained with the Group. There is emphasis on the personal development of group members as well as on increasing their environmental and cultural understanding. Most expeditions incorporate a fieldwork, environmental or community project coupled with a discovery phase to understand the people and the landscape. No previous experience or skills are necessary. The fees range from £200 to £2000 and cover all aspects of the venture including comprehensive insurance. All you need is your own spending money, personal clothing etc. and a sense of humour. Advice given on raising funds.

BSES Expeditions

The Royal Geographical Society, 1 Kensington Gore London SW7 2AR
Tel: 020 7591 3141   Fax: 020 7591 3140
Email:bses@rgs.org   Web: www.bses.org.uk

Founded in 1932 by the late Surgeon Commander G. Murray Levick, a member of Scott's 1910 Antarctic expedition, the Society provides opportunities for young people aged between 16_ and 20 to take part each summer in exploratory projects in far-flung regions. These expeditions create the challenge of adventure in remote and hostile environments, fostering the dedication, companionship and personal initiative so necessary to the spirit of both successful exploration and everyday life.

Traditional venues are the Arctic and sub-Arctic, but in the last few years there have been expeditions also to Kenya, India, Malawi and Kyrghyzstan. Applications have to be made by October of the previous year; final selection is completed in December. Applicants need some knowledge of camping and hill-walking, but the Society looks for young people with a variety of abilities and skills. Individuals are expected to make a contribution to the costs of the expedition and help is given in fund-raising.

Coral Cay Conservation

13th Floor, 125 High Street, Colliers Wood, London SW19 2JG
Tel: 0208 545 7717   Fax: 0870 750 0667
Email: info@coralcay.org   Web: www.coralcay.org

Coral Cay Conservation (CCC) is an award winning, non-profit making British organisation that provides resources to help sustain livelihoods through the protection, restoration and management of fragile coral reef environments and tropical rainforests. CCC is funded through self-financing volunteers who join CCC projects to take an active part in gathering the data used to protect and manage threatened marine and forest environments. CCC recruits volunteers from age sixteen upwards to join expeditions from two to twelve weeks.

Volunteers do not need any previous scientific training or expedition experience as CCC provides full training. The training and research methods pioneered by CCC have been independently reviewed and internationally accredited. Since 1986 hundreds of volunteers have joined CCC each year. With their support CCC has helped establish eight marine and wildlife reserves, including the new Belize Barrier Reef World Heritage Site. Projects currently in the Philippines and Bay Islands of Honduras, with new projects starting in Fiji, American Samoa, Malaysia and Papua New Guinea. CCC regularly holds presentations throughout the country. For more details contact the above.

Dorset Expeditionary Society

Chickerell Road, Weymouth, Dorset DT4 9SY
Tel/Fax: 01305 775599
Email: dorsetexp@wdi.co.uk　　　　**Web: www.dorsetexp.co.uk**

The Dorset Expeditionary Society is a registered charity which promotes safe adventurous opportunities for young people. Expedition Leaders, who are all volunteers, run up to six overseas expeditions each year which are open to anyone throughout the UK and always take place during the academic summer holidays. Team sizes vary from 6 to 24, duration from 3 to 5 weeks, costs from £500 to £2200. Prior selection and training weekends are held. Activities include mountaineering, jungle survival, kayaking, white water rafting, trekking and mountain biking. Past locations include the French and Swiss Alps, Alaska, Bolivia, Canada (British Columbia), China, Dolomites, Ecuador, Iceland, India (Himalayas), Indonesia, Kenya, Mexico, Morocco, Pakistan and Peru.

In addition to the experience of overseas travel and the acquisition of skills in survival in the wilderness areas of the world, expedition team members will also be asked to take responsibility for one crucial element of the expedition, thus developing their own leadership, self-sufficiency and team working skills. The Society provides administrative support, assists with recruitment, provides a database of information and a UK contact service. There is also a mentoring programme to support those starting to organise their own venture. The Society also has a sponsored training programme, organises social events, produces a regular newsletter and has a full programme providing opportunities for disadvantaged youth in the UK.

Explore Worldwide

Tel: 0870 333 4002
1 Frederick Street, Aldershot, Hampshire GU11 1LQ
Email:info@exploreworldwide.com Web:www.exploreworldwide.com
Founded in 1981 now offers small-group adventure travel opportunities in over 100 countries worldwide; volcanoes to glaciers to jungles.

Flying Fish

25 Union Road, Cowes, Isle of Wight, PO31 7TW
Tel: 01983 280641
Email: via website   Web: www.flyingfishonline.com
Flying Fish provides training and work placements for sailors, divers, surfers, windsurfers, kitesurfers, skiers and snowboarders, in Australia, Canada, Greece, Cyprus, Egypt and the UK, leading to professional qualifications from the RYA, AYF, IKO. CSIA, CASI and PADI. No previous experience is required. Some courses are for beginners, others for intermediates and experts. Courses include work experience and lead to paid jobs in Europe, Australia and the South Pacific. ATOL-protected.

Frontier - the Society for Environmental Exploration

50-52 Rivington Street, London EC2A 4QP
Tel: 020 7613 2422   Fax: 020 7613 2992
Email: info@frontier.ac.uk   Web: www.frontier.ac.uk
Frontier is a tropical conservation research organisation carrying out environmental surveys in Madagascar, Tanzania and Vietnam. The data that is collected is used in the setting up of management plans to help preserve some of the world's most threatened habitats. To help carry out the research Frontier look for volunteers to come out on 28 day, 10 or 20 week phases, living and working in a remote area, be it a savanna, tropical forest or marine environment. No technical qualifications are necessary as all training is provided. Volunteers must though have an interest in conservation, be able to work in a team and live under field conditions. Marine volunteers must be qualified divers, although they can also be trained in the field. Training in the field is so extensive that all volunteers are eligible to qualify for a BTEC Advanced Diploma in Tropical Habitat Conservation (on 10 and 20 week expeditions) or a BTEC Certificate in Expedition Management (on 28 day expedition). Many volunteers use the experience to help them follow a career in conservation and overseas development. Expeditions cost from £1,850 (28 days), £2,150 (10 weeks), and £3,800 (20 weeks) plus flights and visas. For a free information pack contact Jenny Darwin at the above address.

Gap Challenge

Black Arrow House, 2 Chandos Road, London NW10 6NF
Tel: 020 8728 7200   **Fax: 020 8961 1551**
Email:welcome@world-challenge.co.uk Web: world-challenge.co.uk

Gap Challenge is part of World Challenge Expeditions who have been providing overseas opportunities for young people for over 15 years. Students aged 18 to 25 can choose between placements in 11 countries, including Australia, Belize, India, Nepal and Tanzania. Each year over 400 students organise their gap year with Gap Challenge. The team applies choice and flexibility over each placement, allowing every potential Gap Challenger to maintain their individuality. There are several start dates a year. Placements last three and six months and include teaching, conservation, carework, eco-tourism and agricultural work with local conservation groups. With a twelve month return flight there is plenty of opportunity for independent travel afterwards. All applicants are required to attend a two-day selection course. These are held throughout the year. There is also an obligatory Skills Training course before departure where Gap Challengers receive information and briefings from qualified staff and a chance to meet ex-Gap Challengers.

Individuals can apply for placements up until a month before departure, so we can accommodate last minute applicants whose plans may have changed. Other opportunities include summer placements as well as exciting Team Challenge expeditions to Borneo, East Africa and South America. While away Gap Challengers are offered advice and support from an in-country agent who is available to help them make the most of their time, as well as a 24 hour emergency back-up system from Gap Challenge in London. Check the Web for full details and to download an information pack.

Global Vision International

Amwell Farmhouse, Nomansland, Wheathampstead, St Albans, Herts AL4 8EJ
Tel: 0870 608 8898   **Fax: 01582 834002**
Email: info@gvi.co.uk   **Web: www.gvi.co.uk**

GVI Expeditions are run in conjunction with governments, world agencies and pioneering charities to provide long term support to critical conservation projects. GVI supply all science and expedition staff as well as the technical equipment to ensure the validity of these programmes well into the future. Current expeditions are supported by 10 to 20 participants at any one time and run throughout the world for periods of 5 to 20 weeks.

Madventurer

Hawthorn House, Forth Banks, Newcastle NE1 3SG
Tel: 0845 121 1996
Email: team@madventurer.com   **Web: www.madventurer.com**

Madventurer organises award winning gap year expeditions in Africa and South America. Gap year Students aged 17 and above take part in 5 week to 3 month development projects before departing on overland adventures. Madventurer's volunteer expeditions take place in Ghana, Kenya, Tanzania, Togo, Uganda, Peru, Bolivia, and Trinidad & Tobago.

Outward Bound Trust

Ullswater, Nr Penrith, Cumbria CA11 0JL
Tel: 0870 513 4227   **Fax: 017684 86405**
Email: enquiries@outwardbound-uk.org Web:www.outwardbound-uk.org

The Outward Bound Trust is the longest standing, most experienced outdoor personal development training organisation in the UK. It has four centres in the UK with a network of 27 voluntary associations and over 250 staff working with 20,000 participants each year. There are also centres in another 30 countries around the world. The Outward Bound Trust only rarely employs people under 21 years, but it offers stimulating courses, many of them outdoors, adventurous and enjoyable, which offer valuable experience in handling different people and problems in an unfamiliar, challenging environment. Outward Bound Expedition courses operate away from the Outward Bound centres and groups form self-sufficient autonomous units walking or sailing, with canoeing and rock climbing included in the programme.

Quest Overseas

The North-West Stables, Borde Hill Estate, Balcombe Road, Haywards Heath, West Sussex RH16 1XP
Tel: 01444 474744   **Fax: 01444 474799**
Email: emailingyou@questoverseas.com   Web:www.questoverseas.com

Applicants must be over 18 years old with relevant interests and skills. We need charismatic, computer literate students with a keen interest in the travel industry, conservation, expeditions and third world issues. Due to demand for these positions we are now only accepting Students who have already participated in a Quest Overseas Project or Expedition.

Quest South America

Quest Overseas pioneered the concept of combining Spanish language training, voluntary work projects and challenging Andean expeditions into all-encompassing three month adventures in South America.

Intensive Spanish Course: 3 weeks. Quito, Ecuador or Sucre, Bolivia.

Voluntary Work Projects: 4 weeks. Rainforest and cloudforest conservation in Ecuador.

Working with children in the district of Villa Maria, Lima, Peru. Animal conservation in   Parque Machia Animal Sanctuary, Chapare, Bolivia.

Expedition: 6 weeks. Andean expedition exploring over 1,000kms of Peru, Chile and Bolivia, from the depths of the Amazon jungle to the breathtaking peaks of Machu Picchu.

Quest Africa

Voluntary Work Projects: 6 weeks. Conservation work in the Kingdom of Swaziland, actively assisting in the conservation of southern African community, nature and game reserves. Experience Tanzanian village life in the Community Development Project.

Expedition: 6 weeks. Encompassing Swaziland, Mozambique, South Africa, Botswana and Zambia, exploring some of the best Africa has to offer. In short, six weeks that will blow your mind!

Participants are required to raise the necessary funds including a significant contribution towards their chosen voluntary work project.

Raleigh International

27 Parsons Green Lane, London SW 4HZ
Tel: 020 7371 8585   Fax: 020 7371 5116
Email: info@raleigh.org.uk   Web: www.raleigh.org.uk

Raleigh International aims to develop young people through challenging community and environmental work on projects and expeditions around the world. Each expedition lasts around 10 weeks and destinations have included Chile, Namibia, Costa Rica, Mongolia and Ghana. The expeditions allow 'venturers' the opportunity to learn new skills and experience new cultures in the remotest parts of the expedition country. Anyone between the ages of 17 and 25 can apply to join an expedition as long as they can swim 200 meters and understand English. All have to attend an introduction weekend and go on to raise funds for the charity.

Sail Training Association (STA)

2A The Hard, Portsmouth PO1 3PT
Tel: 023 9283 2055   Fax: 023 9281 5769
Email: tallships@sta.org.uk
Web: www.sta.org.uk or www.tallships-adventure.com

The Sail Training Association offers young people the opportunity of a life time to sail up to 1,000 miles and visit foreign ports on a two-week adventure on board the STA's Tall Ships PRINCE WILLIAM or STAVROS S NIARCHOS. Adventure voyages are available to all young people between the ages of 16 and 24 with sponsorship available if required. Voyages take place in Northern European Waters, the Canary Islands, Azores or why not join us for the ultimate challenge - a trans Atlantic crossing to the Caribbean! If you want a unique experience and one where you will not have a minute to be bored, get more information from the STA. All voyages qualify for the Duke of Edinburgh Gold Award.

Trekforce Expeditions

34 Buckingham Palace Road London SWIW ORE
Tel: 020 7828 2275   **Fax: 020 7828 2276**
Email: info@trekforce.org.uk   **Web: www.trekforce.org.uk**

Trekforce Expeditions (founded 1990) organizes tough 8 - 20 week conservation and scientific projects in Central and South America and East Malaysia concentrating on endangered rainforests and working with local communities. Our extended programmes of four to five months incorporate expedition teamwork, learning new languages and teaching in rural communities, such as the Kelabit of Sarawak or the Spanish and Mayan speaking communities of Belize. If you are looking for a challenging adventure come and find out more on one of our introduction days. We accept applications throughout the year. Minimum age 18 years. Volunteers are required to fundraise a set target.

World Challenge Expeditions

Black Arrow House, 2 Chandos Road, London NW10 6NF
Tel: 0208 728 7200   **Fax: 0208 961 1551**
Email: welcome@world-challenge.co.uk Web: www.world-challenge.co.uk

Whether you're up to your eyes in exams or planning your time at university, applying for your first job or deciding your future career – perhaps it's time you thought about the benefits of taking a gap year or fitting a gap year placement into your summer holidays. Taking a well structured gap year is a fantastic opportunity for you to gain a sense of self-reliance, confidence and a CV or UCAS form that will stand out from the rest. But more importantly, it's a once-in-a-lifetime chance for you to gain a broader perspective of the world and a true sense of achievement. WCE runs a variety of programmes designed to ensure you make the most of your time out. Ranging from 2-9 months on a Gap Challenge placement in Costa Rica or Tanzania to a 14 day First Challenge expedition in Morocco, all of the programmes will equip you with the skills and experience you'll need to face the challenges ahead. Not only can you fit an expedition into your summer holidays - there are many Gap Challenge placements available over the summer too.

Language courses

If you have applied for a higher education course that includes languages, you may well be hoping to spend part of your gap year, or summer holiday, living in your chosen country. But if you do not see yourself as a linguist you may also benefit from brushing up your French or learning basic Italian in order to add language facility to your portfolio of skills - and the best way to do this is to immerse yourself in the life and culture of the country concerned and join one of the many available courses. In some centres it is also possible to combine language learning with sports and other activities - for example, skiing, art, craft, cookery, wine.

The British Institute of Florence

Piazza Strozzi 2, 50123 Firenze, Italy
Tel: 00 39 055 26778200   **Fax: 00 39 055 26778222**
Email: tbray@britishinstitute.it   **Web: www.britishinstitute.it**

The British Institute of Florence offers an extensive range of courses in Italian Language, Art History, Practical Art and Italian Culture attracting over 700 students from the UK, USA and the rest of the world each year.In addition over 2000 Italians, some as young as 5, come to the Institute each year to participate in English courses and to take the Cambridge English for speakers of other Languages (ESOL) exams. The British Institute of Florence was founded in 1917 with the aim of developing cultural understanding between the UK and Italy through the teaching of their respective languages and cultures and the maintenance in Florence of a library. In 1923 it was granted a Royal Charter and in 1953 was recognised in the Anglo-Italian Cultural Convention as an official representative of British culture in Italy.

Caledonia Languages Abroad

The Clockhouse, Bonnington Mill, 72 Newhaven Road, Edinburgh EH6 5QG
Tel: 0131 621 7721   **Fax: 0131 621 7723**
Email: courses@caledonialanguages.co.uk Web: www.caledonialanguages.co.uk

We offer language courses in over 50 schools worldwide, in Spain, France, Italy, Germany, Portugal, Brazil, Bolivia, Mexico, Peru, Cuba, Costa Rica, Ecuador, Russia and Argentina. We regularly visit our partners to keep up to date with developments and can personally recommend courses based on our own experience. Courses at all levels from beginner to advanced are available all year round. Gap year options include combining languages courses in two or more locations; language with cultural studies from 3-6 months; Spanish plus volunteer work programmes in Bolivia, Peru and Costa Rica. Accommodation in homestay or many other options also arranged. Regular social and cultural activities are included in course fees. Contact us to discuss your interests and to receive a brochure.

CESA Languages Abroad

CESA House, Pennance Road, Lanner, Cornwall, TR16 5TQ
Tel. 01209 211 800   Fax. 01209 211 830
Email: info@cesalanguages.com   Web: www.cesalanguages.com

CESA Languages Abroad offers foreign language courses around the world.
We are founder members of the Year Out Group (see Introduction). Spanish,
French, Italian, German, Russian, Japanese and Chinese are featured in our
main brochure (free on request). Additional language and location options are
offered via the Web or direct from the office.

Programmes include: AS & A2 level preparation (1+ weeks), short and
long term Gap Year courses (4-24+ weeks) and private tuition (1+ weeks)
throughout the year. Whilst students may have GCSE or A level language
ability before booking a course, others are beginners starting from scratch. We
are always happy to discuss the course, college, location and accommodation
options with you and can provide courses leading to language qualifications,
e.g. the DELE in Spain or the DELF diplomas in France. Please email, write or
telephone for details.

Challenge Educational Services

101 Lorna Road, Hove, Sussex BN3 3EL
Tel: 01273 208648   Fax: 01273 220376
Email:enquiries@challengeuk.com   Web:www.challengeuk.com

Challenge Educational Services is a French Language Specialist offering courses
suitable for students of all levels, ages and requirements - with a guarantee of
total immersion into the French language and culture. They specialise in French
university programmes, including the world famous Sorbonne in Paris. In
addition to term and academic year programmes, the universities offer summer
programmes for 4-8 weeks.

Programme fees are fully inclusive of registration fees, accommodation and
board, either in a student residence or in a host family. Challenge can offer French
language programmes to suit all levels, from complete beginners to advanced; for
business or for pleasure, and for any duration from one week to a full academic
year. They also offer specialist programmes such as French plus art in Paris,
specific A level revision programmes and under 18s programmes combining
tuition with a variety of sporting and cultural activities.

Don Quijote International

PO Box 218, Epsom, Surrey KY19 0YF
Tel: 020 8786 8081   Fax: 020 8786 8086 Email:
Email: info@donquijote.co.uk   Web: www.donquijote.org

This company runs Spanish language courses at all levels lasting 1-40 weeks suitable for gap students at eight locations in Spain and Latin America, including Madrid, Seville, Tenerife, Mexico and Peru. On the longer courses students can study in one city only or two or three. As well as intensive language tuition there are optional extras and courses combining business and tourism subjects. Students can stay in host families or in flats. Enquiries and resertvations on the website.

En Famille Overseas

La Maison Jaune, avenue du Stade, 34210 SIRAN, France
UK Tel: 01206 546741 Tel and Fax Frrance: 0033 468914990
Email: marylou.toms@wanadoo.fr Web: www.enfamilleoverseas.co.uk

Established in 1945, En Famille Overseas sends many students each year to stay with host families. The objective is a total immersion in the language for anything from one week to one year.

Opportunities exist to attend small private schools too. Life in another country is very different but always fascinating. Not only do you find out about them, you also find out about yourself. The give and take and excitement of a new situation is challenging, whatever your age, but it is also very fulfilling.

EF International Language Schools

Dudley House, 36-38 Southampton Street, London WC2E 7HF
Tel: 08707 200 735   Fax: 08707 200 767
Email: eflanguages@ef.com   Web: www.ef.com

EF provides foreign language courses in France, Germany, Spain, Italy, Ecuador, China and Russia. Courses start every other Monday and last from two to 52 weeks. In addition to the course, EF also organises accommodation in carefully selected host families or a student residence. Each school offers a wide range of cultural and social activities. EF has designed three programmes specifically for GAP year students:

- **EF Academic Year Abroad**: Spend nine or six exciting months abroad and come home fluent in a new language. An EF Academic Year Abroad is the ideal way to immerse yourself completely in your host country's culture and the most effective way to learn a language.

- **EF Multi-Language Year:** The only programme designed to help you become both multilingual and multicultural in just nine months.

- **Teaching English as a Foreign Language:** Train for the EF Certificate or Diploma in TEFL or for the Trinity Certificate TESOL, then spend a year teaching at one of our schools in China, Indonesia, Thailand or Russia.

If you want to learn a language, discover a new culture and gain valuable skills to impress future employers, please call 08707 200 735 for a free brochure.

Euro Academy Ltd

67 - 71 Lewisham High Street, London SE13 5JX
Tel 020 8297 0505   Fax 020 8297 0984
Email: euroacademy@twinuk.com   Web: www.euroacademy.co.uk

This organisation, established for over 30 years, can arrange all year round homestays and all year courses in France, Germany, Italy, Spain, Portugal, Russia and Ecuador. Most tuition is in small groups. Local coordinators provide a point of contact when abroad. Special gap year courses include German in Berlin, long-term Spanish, art and language in Florence, long-term French from 4, 8 or 12 weeks - all levels. Preparation for French and Spanish diplomas. Protection of an ABTA-bonded company.

Home Language International

Le Coronado, 20 Avenue de Fontuieille, MC98000, Monaco.
Tel:37797 707472   Fax:37797 707471
Email:hli@monaco.mc   Web: www.hli.co.uk

Students live with, and learn from, private teachers on a one-to-one basis. They receive 15, 20 or 25 hours of lessons a week and every effort is made to provide for individual interest and hobbies by careful choice of families. As there is only one student per home, students have no real opportunity to speak their mother tongue, which makes the experience more intensive than group lessons. Qualified teachers are available in France, Germany, Spain, Russia, Italy, Japan, Brazil, China, Egypt, Hungary and many other countries.

International House

106 Piccadilly, London W1J 7NL
Tel: 020 7518 6982
Email: studyabroad@ihlondon.co.uk   Web: www.ihlondon.com

This is one of the largest independent teacher training and language institute in London and also has 120 schools around the world. It is well-known for its teacher training courses, including one or 4 week courses particularly useful for gap year students. Courses in French, German, Italian and Spanish are also offered. Contact the Affiliate Network Department for information concerning International House centres abroad.

LANACOS Language Courses Abroad

64 London Road, Dunton Green, Sevenoaks, Kent TN13 2UG
Tel:01732 462309   Fax:01732 450192
Email:languages@lanacos.com   Web:www.lanacos.com

"The limits of your language are the limits of your world". Experience quality language courses on location in Europe, Latin America, and Japan. Residential language courses checked, reviewed and improved on by LANACOS guarantee the gap-year student maximum results in a minimum amount of time.

Language Studies International

19-21 Ridgmount Street, London WC1E 7AH
Tel: 020 7467 6506　　　　**Fax: 020 7323 1736**
Email: fl@lsi.edu　　　　　**Web:www.lsi.edu**

Formed in 1965, LSI now has nineteen language schools in eleven countries, offering quality language training programmes to students from all over the world. Therer are centres in France, Spain, Italy, Germany, Switzerland, Latin America, China, Japan and Russia. Language training is provided through a wide range of both short and long term courses, designed to ensure that participants can communicate effectively in social, educational and professional situations. Language and culture are closely linked, which is why all our centres organise a social programme to allow you to discover your host country, practice the language and enjoy yourself.

SIBS

Beech House, Commercial Road, Uffculme, Cullompton, Devon EX15 3EB
Tel: 01884 841330　　　　**Fax: 01884 841377**
Email: trish@sibs.co.uk　　　**Website: www.sibs.co.uk**

SIBS Ltd offers a complete service for those wishing to study a foreign language in the country where it is spoken. Advice and information given on numerous private language schools. Clients can be assissted in selecting the course best suited to their needs. Tutition and accommodation are booked as required. We can also arrange ISIS travel insurance and help arrange travel if required.

Fine art, design and animation

Art History Abroad

179c New Kings Road, London SW6 4SW
Tel: 020 7731 2231　　　　**Fax: 020 7731 2456**
Email: info@arthistoryabroad.com　　**Web: www.arthistoryabroad.com**

AHA's six week course is a lifetime experience, traveling throughout Italy studying at first hand many masterpieces of Italian art which form the foundations of western civilization. Art History Abroad has pulled out all the stops to ensure that this programme is second to none. We continue to break new ground, always looking to improve this intoxicating recipe of education, exhilaration, great times and life changing moments. Venice (10 nights), Verona (4 nights), Florence (10 nights), Siena (4 nights), Naples (4 nights) and Rome (10 nights). We make day excursions to at least six of the following towns: Padua, Vicenza, Ravenna, Modena, Urbino, PIsa, San Gimignano, Arezzon, Orvieto, Pompeii and Tivoli.

Escape Studios

Escape Studios, Shepherds West, Rockley Road, London W14 0DA
Tel: 020 7348 1920   **Fax: 020 7348 1921**
Email: info@escapestudios.co.uk   **Web: www.escapestudios.co.uk**

A specialist provider of computer animation training at all levels. The wide range of courses includes a five-day visual effects introductory course, described as an ideal place to start for those unsure of which area of computer graphics and animation they wish to pursue. Learning Days are held on the last Saturday of every month.

John Hall Venice

12 Gainsborough Road, Ipswich IP4 2UR
Tel: 01473 251223   **Fax: 01473 288009**
Email: info@johnhallvenice.co.uk   **Web: www.johnhallvenice.co.uk**

Begun in 1965 by John Hall, the Pre-University Course for Gap Year students offers an introduction to Italian and European civilisation- from the classical past to Today. It is conducted by a team of world-class experts and includes not only art, architecture and sculpture but also music, cinema, industrial design, literature, photography, drawing and painting and Italian language. Fundamental to the aim and ideals of the Course is spending a meaningful period of time in one city - six weeks in Venice. This allows a residential style of living. Students feel at home in, and get to know an Italian city in some depth, not as sight-seers in transit.

Usually there are about 45 students on the Course, mainly British but with a regular American presence. Together with a few students from other countries- Holland, Sweden, France, Germany, Spain, Australia, New Zealand, Canada-this adds an international dimension to our community.

KLC School of Design Ltd

Unit 503, The Chambers, Chelsea Harbour, London SW10 0XF
Tel: 020 7376 3377   **Fax: 020 7376 7807**
Email: info@klc.co.uk   **Web: www.klc.co.uk**

This school runs a ten week Certificate course in Interior Decoration, open to people of all ages, but especially appropriate to interested school leavers who are either considering going on to a higher education design course or wish to learn more about the subject. It does not claim to provide a full design training but it can offer a foundation for work or study in this area, as well as a taster of a wide range of interior design issues and techniques, from planning room layouts, assembling a professional sample board, sketching , curtain making and decorative paint finishes. The course is structured to include lectures, hands-on practice in workshops, visits to specialist showrooms and historical houses.

The cost for 2003 is £3700 plus VAT. KLC also runs a one-year Diploma course as well as a number of short, specialist courses. Full details of the syllabus and a prospectus from the above address.

Studio Art Centers International (SACI) - Florence

Palazzo dei Cartelloni, Via Sant'Antonino, 11, 50123 Florence, Italy
Tel: (011)39 055 289948   Fax: (011) 39 055 2776408
Email: info@saci-florence.org   Web: www.saci-florence.org

SACI was founded in 1975 to offer U.S. university level studies in Florence, Italy. Completely accredited programs for serious students seeking excellence in studio art, art history, art conservation and Italian cultural and language studies are offered in 40 different disciplines at all levels. SACI's facilities are located in the historic center of Florence and include the Palazzo dei Cartelloni (17th Century landmark), Graduate Center and newly opened Design Center; all buildings are within walking distance of major monuments, the central market and student apartments.

Intensive Summer programs include Archeological Conservation courses on the Island of Elba as well as two terms in Florence. Year/Semester abroad programs are also available to Gap Year students and include special programs in Architecture. For more information please contact the SACI administrative office in NY: saci@iie.org.

Sports instructor awards

Altitude Futures

UK address: 71 Claramount Road, Heanor, Derbyshire DE75 7HS
Swiss address: Case Postale 55, 1936-Verbier, Switzerland
Tel: 07800 737948
Email:info@altitude-extreme.com   Web: www.altitude-futures.com

Altitude Futures is offering you the chance to become a fully qualified ski instructor. Change your skiing for life! Learn how to teach, improve your leadership and communication skills, learn French and have lots of fun! Whether you are on a gap year out from University, looking to take a career break or wanting to change your career this is the course for you. Offering quality training and assessment with British Coaches in one of the worlds leading ski resorts.

We are based in the world renowned resort of Verbier in Switzerland and are offering a 10 week ski instructor training and development programme that will give you an internationally recognised qualification and open up worldwide career opportunities .We work closely with our partner company Altitude Snowsport School who provide opportunities for practical teaching experience as well as a host of highly qualified instructors and coaches.

The International Academy

St Hilary Court, Copthorne Way, Culverhouse Cross, Cardiff CF5 6ES
Tel: 029 206 72500   Fax: 02920 672510
Email: info@theinternationalacademy.com
Web: www.theinternationalacademy.com

As a sport and travel specialist we focus on providing enjoyable experiences that generate an opportunity to develop life-long skills and to further education in its broadest context. We offer gap-year programmes that allow students to gain professional sport instructor qualifications at some of the world's most exotic locations including Canada, America, the Seychelles and New Zealand. These programmes bring new and exciting possibilities to young people and create memorable life-changing experiences. Delegates can take part in our residential courses ranging from four to twelve weeks and train to qualify in sporting-disciplines including skiing, snowboarding, scuba-diving and whitewater rafting. The courses are awarded by the relevant national governing bodies and are recognised worldwide, and we can cater for all abilities. Our courses include flights, transfers, half-board accommodation, tuition, learning manuals, examination fees and the services of an International Academy representative.

Nonstopski

79 Leathwaite Road, London, SW11 6RN
Tel: 0870 241 80 70
Email: info@nonstopski.com   Web: www.nonstopski.com

NONSTOPSKI is a family-run company with a passion for the mountains, snow and adventure. We offer a friendly personal service and aim to provide you with the experience of a lifetime in some of the world's most stunning scenery. Established in January 2002, the 2004/05 season will be our third season running ski and snowboard instructor courses and improvement programmes in Canada. Due to high demand are now offering 11-week ski and snowboard instructor courses at Red Mountain and Banff. We were recently rated the 'Most Enterprising New Ski Business' by Peter Hardy, author of the Good Ski and Snowboard Guide, after he visited us in Fernie and experienced a couple of days with our professional coaches and had learnt about the variety of training incorporated into our programmes.

Peak Leaders Gap Year Ski & Snowboard Instructor Programmes

Peak Leaders, Mansfield, Strathmiglo, Fife KY14 7QE
Tel: 01337 860 079   Fax: 01337 868 176
Email: info@peakleaders.com   Web: www.peakleaders.com

Peak Leaders is a highly experienced family business running 4 ski and snowboard instructor courses - Canada (1. Banff / Lake Louise; 2.

Whistler) 3. New Zealand and 4. Argentina. Our aim is to provide quality, safe, gap year and time out training world wide through structured programmes of learning. As trainees you learn to be ski or snowboard instructors with modules in first aid, mountain safety, avalanche awareness, team / leader management, informal French or Spanish language (Canada & Argentina only). You also benefit hugely from living in a different culture.

The theme of Peak Leaders courses is personal development giving you skills for employment and for life. Courses are great fun, inspiring, life directing and life changing. Courses deliver an excellent range of vocational and transferable skills providing a strong basis for gaining employment in similar or complementary fields. Whether you go into the industry or take a different path in life the skills you gain on a Peak Leaders course will stay with you.

The structure of our courses is typically, as follows: First day, a welcome talk from your local team with programme overview followed by a mountain familiarisation tour in the afternoon. You will then, with your instructors, plunge into technical enhancement training, learn teaching principals, watch video playback sessions, experience team leader building and instructor exam preparation. You will also get first aid and avalanche awareness courses. The back country taster / module provides you with transceivers, shovels, probes and the knowledge of how to use them... the kind of experience all instructors should have. With shadowing in the ski school, advanced training and optional freestyle, plus of course all that partying, you are into week 11 before you know it! The course ends with the traditional farewell party before we fly back to the UK. Many of our trainees are now instructing worldwide – this year, just in Sunshine in the Rockies there are 12 past trainees working in ski school, to say nothing of those working in Lake Louise, Whistler etc..... Join us! For further info please do not hesitate to contact us or check out our website.

Ski Le Gap

P.O.Box 474, 220 Chemin Wheeler, Mont Tremblant, Quebec J0T 1Z0
Brochure line: 0800 328 0345 or direct Tel: 001 819 429 6599
Email: info@skilegap.com   Web: www.skilegap.com

Ski le Gap is the ORIGINAL ski/snowboard instructors' course specifically designed for gap-year students from Britain. Created in 1994 by Beryl Puddifer, its aim is to provide young people with the ultimate gap-year experience. Beryl worked as the Principal of a private British college for 15 years and has been organizing trips for British students visiting Canada for over 25 years. She lives in Canada and actively manages and supervises the programme.

Spending the winter season at Ski le Gap provides the opportunity to gain practical qualifications whilst experiencing a new culture and learning a second language – all this in a Canadian winter wonderland of blue skies, six-foot snow drifts, ice palaces and carnivals, and temperatures that can dip below –30 degrees centigrade...

Ski le Gap has developed two options for gap-year students: the three-month main programme and the four-week Mini-Gap course. The main programme runs from January through March and students spend three jam-packed months gaining the experience of a lifetime. We put as much emphasis upon developing exciting and dynamic après-ski activities as we do upon offering the most innovative and challenging snow programme in Canada. Students participate in French conversation lessons; play ice hockey on their own outdoor rink; extreme snowshoe down mountainsides; visit Quebec City, Montreal & Ottawa, and much, much more. All activities offered in the main programme are included in the cost of the course.

The four week Mini-Gap course is for students with prior ski or snowboarding skills who want an intensive instructors' course specifically to gain a Level I certification. This course is arranged at the beginning of the season in Canada in order to enable qualified students to have the opportunity to teach at the mountain over the Christmas and New Year period. Enrolment is limited. This is a very focused course: it is fun, intense and exciting, but it is not for complete beginners! Ski le Gap is situated at Mont Tremblant in the picturesque French-speaking province of Quebec and students live campus-style in a charming old hunting lodge at the edge of a lake.

United Kingdom Sailing Academy

West Cowes, Isle of Wight, PO31 7PQ
Tel: 01983 294941   **Fax:01983 295938**
Email: info@uksa.org   **Web: www.uksa.org**

If you have always wanted to try watersports, enjoyed the taste of a life afloat on a previous holiday, or are already hooked on watersports, the UKSA has a range of training options which could provide a gap year with a difference and even lead to a career in the worldwide marine industry. It has superb, modern facilities with residential accommodation.

There are two main options. One is a six week fast track course to become a professional instructor in either windsurfing or dinghy sailing. The other is a twelve week multi-discipline course covering instruction in dinghy sailing, windsurfing and kayaking. Dinghy and kayaking options are taught at Cowes, with windsurfing taught at the Academy's campys in Barbados. This also gvies the opportunity to gain the recognised PADI diving qualification to teach sub-aqua. Fees start from £3000 and include all tuition, accommodation, flights and food in the UK.

For students interested in bigger boats there is a seventeen week yachting programme which qualifies you to crew leisure yachts around the world. Training costs around £9000 and includes all tuition, accommodation and food. The Academy runs its own in-house careers agency which can help students find work during their vacations. It holds monthly open days. UKSA is a regstered charity supported by the Lister Trust.

World Class Skiing

42 Green Dell Way, Leverstock Green, Hemel Hempstead HP3 8PQ
Tel: 0845 230 1520
Email: info@worldclassskiing.net   Web: www.world-class-skiing.com

Qualify as a BASI instructor in your Gap Year. Our 10-week program at Mayrhofen culminates in students taking their British Association of Snowsports Instructors (BASI) Grade 3 Alpine certification that opens up a lifetime of skiing opportunity and is a foundation of a career in professional skiing. This GAP program is the best introduction to the world of professional ski instruction ever. Packed with the best training, performance coaching, practical ski school experience, language schooling and lots more, you are guaranteed a season of fun, adventure and learning.

Food and wine

Le Cordon Bleu Culinary Arts Institute

114 Marylebone Lane, London W1U 2HH
Tel: 020 7935 3503   Fax: 020 7935 7621
Email: london@cordonbleu.co.uk   Web:www.cordonbleu.co.uk

The school runs an extensive programme of courses - everything from a one day class to a nine month diploma. Particularly suitable for gap year students is the four week Essentials course held every July and September. Successful students are awarded a certificate and many employers recruit direct from the school.

CookAbility

CookAbility, Sherlands, 54 Stonegallows, Taunton, Somerset TA1 5JS
Tel: 07944 909105 or 01823 461374
Email: cookability@hotmail.com   Web: www.residentialcookery.com

Do you want to learn how to cook? We can help you on our five-day fast track residential course. You cook and eat everything from canapes to casseroles, risotto to roulade, pot roast to pavlova --and much more besides!

The courses are designed to suit individual skills and needs and students receive a certificate on completing the course which can lead to employment in many areas. Some of our students are completing their Duke of Edinburgh

Award Residential Qualification at Gold Standard and others go on to be Chalet cooks, nannies, au pairs or very well fed self-catering undergraduates! Come and cook with us for a fun and flexible five days and leave with a confidence in your ability to cook which will last a lifetime. Courses cost from £340.

Edinburgh School of Food and Wine

The Coach House, Newliston, Edinburgh EH29 9EB
Tel:0131 333 5001   **Fax: 0131 335 3796**
Email: school@cookerycompany.com   **Web: www.cookerycompany.com**

Jill Davidson's School offers courses from foundation level to 'cordon bleu' standard cookery. Courses of particular interest to gap year students are: a one week survival course for independent living run in June, the five week Chalet Cook course, run mainly in the autumn and winter, and the full-length Diploma, a six month intensive course run from January - end June and which includes business topics; There are many opportunities to work freelance and the School works closely with agencies offering freelance employment, for example in ski chalets, directors' dining rooms, yachts and shooting and fishing lodges. There is also a one week Survival course for those leaving home for the first time.

Leiths School of Food and Wine

21 St Alban's Grove, London W8 5BP
Tel: 020 7229 0177   **Fax: 020 7937 5257**
Email: info@leiths.com   **Website: www.leiths.com**

Leiths School of Food and Wine was established in 1975 to provide professional training for career cooks and short courses for amateurs. The School provides comprehensive theoretical and practical teaching, either qualifying students to enter the food and wine business and begin a rewarding career, or simply to instil a lasting love of food and wine. There is commitment to classical techniques and methods, but with a fresh and modern approach. Professional courses range from the Diploma, completed in six or nine months, to the one month Basic Certificate in Practical Cookery, particularly suitable for Gap Year students and school leavers, many of whom work in chalets or shooting lodges. For the enthusiastic amateur we offer daytime courses ranging from a Saturday morning demonstration to a one month advanced course. We have evening classes in both practical cookery and wine appreciation and classes for corporate hospitality groups. Gift vouchers are available. Our successful agency, Leiths List, places cooks and chefs in permanent and temporary positions both in the UK and worldwide.

Tante Marie School of Cookery

Woodham House, Carlton Road, Woking, Surrey GU21 4HF
Tel: 01483 726957   **Fax: 01483 724173**
Email: info@tantemarie.co.uk   **Web: www.tantemarie.co.uk**

In addition to its career-orientated Cordon Bleu Diploma courses, the school offers an 11 week Certificate course and a Four week Essential Skills Course which have proved very popular with gap year students. These courses may be of particular value to those who wish to travel or to work in ski chalets on yachts and to gain temporary employment during their gap year. The cost of the Certificate course, which begins every September, January and April, is £4050 inclusive of VAT. The Essentials skills course runs throughout the year at a cost of £1700. The school also offers 1 and 2 week Beginners Courses held during the Summer holiday periods. The cost for this course is £450 for one week or £775 for 2 weeks. Full details available from the School Secretary.

Business and secretarial skills

Oxford Business College

1st Floor Kings Mead House, Oxpens Road, Oxford OX1 1RX
Tel: 01865 791908   Email: enquiries@oxfordbusinesscollege.co.uk
Web: www.oxfordbusinesscollege.co.uk

PA training plus paid work placement; Office and Computer skills (a gap year option with 4 months training and 2 months paid work placement); Office skills (gap year option, with 2 months training and 1 month paid work placement)

Oxford Media & Business School

Rose Place, St Aldates, Oxford OX1 1SB
Tel: 01865 240963
Email: courses@oxfordbusiness.co.uk   Web: www.oxfordbusiness.co.uk

Gap Year 'Life Skills' course, including IT and Communication skills. Help with finding temping work through OMBS Careers Direct placement bureau. Intensive Graduate Programme: practical work skills – IT, business, career development.

Queen's Business & Secretarial College

24 Queensberry Place, London SW7 2DS
Tel: 020 7589 8583   Fax: 020 7823 9915
Email: info@qbsc.ac.uk   Web: www.qbsc.ac.uk

Business and computer skills are invaluable for university, for work during a gap year and for your career following graduation. Queen's offers courses of one to three terms and short, intensive, modular courses throughout the year. Courses include keyboarding, shorthand, wordprocessing (Word), spreadsheets (Excel), database (Access), presentation package (Powerpoint) and desktop publishing (Pagemaker), the Internet, Email and web page design. Business communication and administration are also covered and career development is an integral part of the course.

St James's & Lucie Clayton College

4 Wetherby Gardens, London SW5 0JN
Tel: 020 7373 3852   **Fax: 020 7370 3303**
Email: information@sjlccollege.co.uk   **Web: www.sjlccollege.co.uk**

Many individuals now include a course as part of their structured gap year as well as travel and fun. One area that has grown in popularity is the acquisition of business skills; by learning keyboarding and commercial IT skills, a student can find temporary office jobs and will find the skills invaluable for university essay writing and for their future career. St James's & Lucie Clayton College offers a number of courses for gap year students; the One Term Gap Course, offered in September, January & April covers three essential areas – commercial IT with keyboard training, practical business studies and personal development ranging from interview techniques to self defence. Short intensive touch typing and IT courses start every Monday and last from one to six weeks & prove particularly popular with male gap year students. The College's associated recruitment consultancy can help to find temporary assignments which can offer attractive rates of pay.

Studying in Australia

IDP Education Australia (UK)

191-199 Thomas Street, Haymarket, Sydney, NSW 2000 Australia
Tel: 00 61 2 8260 3300   **Fax: 00 61 2 8260 3311**
Email: studentservices@idp.com   **Web: www.idp.com**

Represented in 100 locations around the world, IDP is an independent not-for-profit organisation, owned by 38 prestigious universities in Australia. We offer impartial advice on more than 600 prestigious educational institutions offering a choice of over 16,000 courses from secondary school pathway programs to a host of excellent and rewarding vocational education and university qualifications. Please note that this organisation no longer operates a UK office.

CIEE Council Exchanges

1st Plus Ltd, Rosedale House, Rosedale Road, Richmond TW9 2SZ
Tel: 0208 939 9057   **Fax: 0208 332 7858**
Email: info@istplus.com   **Web: www.istplus.com**

CIEE is an international organisation concerned with language learning and cultural exchange services. Four international programs are available to UK applicants: **Internship USA** - Work in the USA in an internship placement; **Professional Career Training USA** - Professional career training in the USA; **Work and Travel Australia** - Work and Travel in Australia; **Work & Travel USA** - Work & Travel in the USA.**Other study opportunities**

The English-Speaking Union

Dartmouth House, 37 Charles Street, London W1J 5ED
Tel: 020 7529 1571   Fax: 020 7495 6108
Email: esu@esu.org   Web: www.esu.org

The English-Speaking Union administers scholarships to enable school leavers in the UK to spend either two or three terms in an American/Canadian boarding school after their A levels. Scholarships may be for a full academic year of three terms, or for two terms from January to June. The scholarship provides board and tuition. Travelling, visa and other expenses are borne by the student. Full details from the ESU Education Department.

Other opportunities

Peter Kirk Memorial Scholarship

The Secretary, 17 St. Paul's Rise, Addingham, Ilkley LS29 0QD
Tel: 01943 839210
Email: mail@kirkfund.org.uk   Web:www.kirkfund.org.uk

These scholarships were founded to commemorate the work of the late Sir Peter Kirk who led the first British team in the European Parliament. Their purpose is to enable suitably qualified young people aged 18-24 to undertake a two to three-month independent study project in one or more countries in Europe. Candidates choose their own subjects for study. About 12 scholarships are offered each year. The value of each is not less than £900. Scholars are expected to provide some finance themselves. Applicants need not be linguists provided that they can converse adequately in the countries they propose to visit. Scholars are expected to complete their projects within 18 months of their award and to write a report within four months of their return. Closing date for applications is mid-February; interviews take place in March/April.

Post Graduate Year in Europe

American School in Switzerland, CH6926 Montagnola-Lugano, Switzerland
Tel: 00 41 91 9946471   Fax 00 41 91 9932979
Email: administration@tasis.ch

The Post Graduate Year of TASIS, The American School in Switzerland is a challenging, educational experience in Europe for high school graduates who would like an interim year before going on to college. Founded in 1956, TASIS is the oldest American boarding school in Europe, with a sister school in England. TASIS is widely recognized as one of the finest schools in Europe. Each year, TASIS schools and summer programs attract over 2,400 students representing more than 40 nationalities who share in a caring, family-style international community. The Post-Graduate Year, established in 1965, enrolls a select group of students who wish to participate in a unique educational opportunity, which draws on the academic strengths of TASIS and the cultural resources of Europe.

Year Out Drama

Stratford-upon-Avon College, Stratford-upon-Avon, CV37 9QR
Tel: 01789 266 245   **Fax: 01789 267 524**
Email: info@yearoutdrama.com   **Web: www.yearoutdrama.com**

Year Out Drama provides intensive, practical drama courses, led by expertss in professionally equipped performance spaces. Courses opffer close links with the RSC and students benefit from working with theatre professionals from varying disciplines, including Acting Techniques, Voice, Movement, Directing, Text Study and Performance. Students perform at the Edinburgh Festival.

Webguide to gap year planning

The following checklist includes a small selection of websites, arranged by key research themes:

- Possible starting points for research
  www.theaward.org - see Thinking about your gap year
  www.thesite.org - see Gap year
  www.yearoutgroup.org
  www.gapyear.com
  www.shu.ac.uk - see Gap year guide

- Thinking about earning during a gap year
  www.suzylamplugh.org/worldwise - see Visa and other advice
  www.yearoutgroup.org
  www.yini.org.uk
  www.theaward.org
  www.fco.gov.uk
  www.back-packer-uk.com - see Job Network and Visa information
  www.gapyear.com

- Thinking about doing voluntary work - UK or elsewhere
  www.theaward.org/gapyear
  www.intervol.org.uk
  www.yearoutgroup.org.
  www.gap.org.uk
  www.worldwidevolunteering.org.uk
  www.do-it.org.uk
  www.shu.ac.uk - see Gap year guide, volunteering

- Planning to travel independently
  www.statravel.co.uk - see Travelling solo
  www.fco.gov.uk - see Backpackers & independent travellers
  www.backpacker-uk.com
  www.gapyear.com

- Planning to join a structured programme
  www.theaward.org - see Join a structured work experience scheme
  www.yini.org.uk - The Year in Industry site
  www.thesite.org
  www.raleigh.org.uk

- Visiting a promotional event
  www.gapyearfairs.co.uk
  www.yearoutgroup.org - see Events

- Health and safety essentials
  www.planetwise.net
  www.fco.gov.uk/knowbeforeyougo - packed with important information
  and tips - 220 partners support the 'know before you go' campaign
  www.masta.info - essential information on minding your health abroad
  www.suzylamplugh.org/worldwise - plenty of useful information including
  'dealing with culture shock' and cultural information
  www.carolinesrainbowfoundation.org.uk - for backpackers in Australia
  www.dh.gov.uk - go to the UK Deptartment for Health's health advice for
  travellers section
  **Loads of essential info including how to get free health treatment both
  inside and outside the EU.**
  www.statravel.co.uk go to Gap year essentials
  www.cdc.gov go to Travellers health

- Flights & travel details
  www.gapwork.com
  www.statravel.co.uk
  www.ukpa.gov.uk - UK Passport office

- Travel Insurance - don't travel without it
  www.gapwork.com
  www.statravel.co.uk
  www.backpacker-uk.com
  www.insureandgo.com

- Financeand budgeting issues
  www.gapwork.com
  www.fco.gov.uk go to Travel money
  www.gapyear.com

- Booking accommodation
  www.gapwork.com
  www.backpacker-uk.com

- Keeping in touch while you're away
  www.csjournal.co.uk - ISCO Careerscope travel diary facility, free for two
  weeks, then £20 per year
  www.statravel.co.uk
  www.gapwork.com
  www.suzylamplugh/worldwise
  www.fco.gov.uk

- Where to get help if things go wrong - contact points and organisations
  www.suzylamplugh.org/worldwise
  www.fco.gov.uk

Support and placement providers

Nine: Webguide and index

151

Nine: Webguide and index